For Mum, who built herself a grotto,
and Shelley Duvall.

JEN CALLEJA

GOBLIN-HOOD

GOBLIN AS A MODE

First published in 2024
by Rough Trade Books

First Edition

ISBN 978-1-914236-45-7

Design by Craig Oldham, Eliza Hart
Printed in England

'Man, I've got to get back into mischief-
writing. Writing stuff that I know no one else
will approve of, just for me, because I think
it's neat or I want to chase something down.
Writing is always easier when you think
of it as mischief.'
—Tim Clare, X, 23 March 2022

Dennis: ...What are some of your 'likes'?
Charlie: Uh, ghouls.
Mac: Son of a bitch. What are you talking
about now?
Charlie: You know, funny little green ghouls.
Dennis: What, like in movies? In cartoons?
Charlie: Little green ghouls, buddy!
—"The Waitress Is Getting Married" (2009),
It's Always Sunny in Philadelphia

Mages & Monsters Master (Shirley): Should I
do my goblin thing or should I play it safe?
Bob: I don't know what you're talking about.
—"Loft in Bedslation" (2021), *Bob's Burgers*

CANNIBALISM
MISCHIEF
SEX
MUSIC
PUPPETS
DISGUISES
GREED
OUBLIETTES
PERVERSION
& GRIEF
AWAIT....

In March 2020, right at the start of the pandemic, Rough Trade Books published my pamphlet memoir-essay **Goblins**, a proto-text for this book. In December 2022, 'goblin mode' was voted Oxford Word of the Year through a public vote. Coincidence?

The BBC article reporting on the popularity of the choice said, 'many of us can feel a little goblin-like occasionally.' Casper Grathwohl, president of Oxford Languages, who was quoted in the article, said, 'the strength of the response highlights how important our vocabulary is to understanding who we are and processing what's happening to the world around us.'

Defining a goblin is tricky: 'they are ascribed conflicting abilities, temperaments, and appearances depending on the story' and can be anything from 'household spirits to malicious, bestial thieves', often having 'magical abilities similar to a fairy or demon, such as the ability to shapeshift'. How would I define "goblin"? I, like many others, consider it an umbrella term. Anything that behaves mischievously and in its own best interest, that is bold and all body, could be a goblin. We can also be made into goblins, stalked by goblins, whether we like it or not. Some things are out of our control.

CONTENTS

GROT

I'd finally hedged the vines of the duvet yet
wake washed-up on a bed of soil
leather mushrooms sprouting from my leather jacket
denim toadstools spreading across my jeans
phosphorescent spores emit in heartbeat puffs
from my fingertips
I tawt I taw a puddy tat with eyes of green but failed
to clock the landslide from the never-ending rain
roll over onto a mud path to Old Raw Gill
a waterfall long lacking its cascade
soon hear water prosperous, blink at a sparkling screen
a portal right out of here.

GREEN

ON EMBLEMATIC EMERALD

As a rule, I always look for green objects in charity and antique shops. It's a particular kind of green I have in mind, a kind of deep jade, or, if made of glass or plastic, emerald. It's so I have one particular thing to search for among the junk rather than aimlessly browsing; it's a microcosm of how I experience the whole world all at once and often need a key to navigate it. This game-for-one is inspired by the film *Return to Oz*, the 1985 non-musical and not-really-a-sequel sequel to *The Wizard of Oz*. In the film, the Nome King has turned the citizens of the Emerald City into stone, trapped Ozma—Princess of Oz—inside the mirror world, and transformed King Scarecrow into a green ornament, which the Nome King has hidden in his cavernous ornament room. Dorothy Gale and her friends the Gump, Jack Pumpkinhead and Tik-Tok the clockwork soldier travel to Nome Mountain to demand the Nome King return the emeralds he's stolen from the Emerald City and de-stone the people of Oz. But they're no match for him—he imprisons Dorothy and takes away her gang of adoring misfits, secretly greenifying them for his collection. The Nome King wants to play a game. He tells Dorothy she can walk around his hall of objects to find her friends, without her knowing that they are green. She must place her hands on the object she thinks might be a friend and shout, '*OZ!*' If she's right, they will transform back. She has three guesses, and each wrong guess makes the heavens roll with thunder. She picks a green object by chance, guesses correctly, and goes on to release many friends. King Scarecrow is a huge emerald, clearly someone precious. I have a memory of finding a piece of green sea glass with my grandad that was so perfect, a smooth green pebble like a big gemstone, but I can't remember if it was real or if I dreamed it, or if I lost it and had dreams where I found it again. We had a set of Disney encyclopaedias growing up that a family friend had given us, and I was obsessed with a set of pages that displayed all the varieties of precious stones—pebble-sized and neatly lined up on the display case page. I think I loved some of them so much I scribbled over them, like when you use a coin on a scratch card in the hope of winning treasure.

After everyone is freed, the Nome King is brought down by Dorothy's pet chicken Billina, who drops an egg into the King's hollow eye socket—'Don't you know' the Nome King booms sadly, 'eggs are poison to gnomes.' The claymation here is terrifying, the grown-huge King, who harnesses the power of the mountain rock, melts in fire, briefly holding onto himself in the form of a fracturing skull before his final collapse. (He looks like he's been hit by the 'malevolent green' torpedo Todd McEwen mentions in his essay about seeing 20,000 *Leagues Under the Sea* as a kid, rather than an egg—McEwen is also taken by the film's monster squid: 'just a big marionette'.)

'Eggs kill the Nome King? I killed the Nome King!' This is how Doug Aberle begins his charming homemade video about creating the clay animation for this and other sequences in *Return to Oz,* showing the four agonising attempts he needed to make the Nome King's crumbling death work. Claymation really sets a film in a particular time, like any technological advancement in film does—puppets with visible strings, shonky CGI. Instagram comedian Claire Manning does a skit about a fictional 80s children's film, a send-up of *Labyrinth* and possibly *Return to Oz* called Sewer Town complete with little songs where the main character's parents are kidnapped by goblins and there's 'randomly claymation'.

The Nome King in *Return to Oz* abducted the citizens of the Emerald City, and the King of England stole the Green Man. In her essay "The Kidnap of the Green Man by the King", poet and essayist Rebecca Tamás speaks of how 'disturbed' she felt to see the image of the Green Man (who we find everywhere here in Hastings, where we moved three years ago, and who looks like the Nome King) on the coronation invitation of King Charles and Queen Camilla. I admit I can only think of the Royal Family as *Spitting Image* puppets. My imaginary friend growing up was Lovejoy, the fictional antiques dealer, and when *Spitting Image* ended they gave the actor who played him, Ian McShane, his puppet doppelgänger: 'I used to have it in a canvas chair in L.A.,' McShane said in an interview, 'with full-size leather jacket propped on top, like a work of art. Over the years, the puppet crumbled beneath it rather like a modern version of Dorian Gray.' Tamás acknowledges that the inclusion of the Green Man is a nod to Charles' self-image as an 'eco-King', but argues that it's grossly inappropriate because the Green Man, with links to May Day and Robin Hood and the commons, is 'a figure of folklore that is tricksy, rebellious and powerful' and Charles and Camilla are massively wealthy landlords. Tamás ends her essay by placing a kind of curse on the King: 'I hope that the Green Man's kidnapped image will flicker out, freeing itself from the misguided invitations, escaping through the haze of bunting and confetti, to haunt the King and his coronation, and to haunt his reign beyond.' Her bad spell continues: 'I hope that its green leaf-ridden voice might echo in the thicket, the river, the hedge and the wood, to remind Charles that nothing lasts—that everything, however old, however powerful, will burn down to ash and fall away.'

Two of my favourite green men are Alistair Green and Anthony Green. Alistair Green (does he ever get called Ali G, I wonder, after the tracksuited demon?) is a comedian and actor who posts videos on Instagram of him playing cringeworthy characters such as moaners from middle England who could be a new version of *Monty Python's* troglodyte Britons with hankies on their heads (did you know that Terry Jones wrote *Labyrinth*?), inept and posh social media influencers, and an array of desperate and unself-aware men. His general persona is a guy who's a bit of a killjoy who talks to camera from his generic white flat and spends his weekends sending dispatches of himself being miserable in public and mocking local gentrification. One of his best creations is a spoof of what *might* be BrewDog ('punks' who rescinded the London Living Wage from their staff and tried to sue anyone that used the word punk in their branding) about a fictional microbrewery fronted by 'Matt' and 'Matt'. One Matt used the profits from his buy-to-let properties to invest in the business, and the other Matt brings his experience as a senior creative at Saatchi & Saatchi (Goblin & Goblin). They reveal at the end that they sold the majority of the company to Budweiser (remember those frogs? *Bud-weis-errr*) for a hundred million, and that Matt can only see his kids every other weekend. Every Halloween, Green reposts a video where he plays the 'night goblin.' A pale and inexplicably shirtless Green enters the bedroom of a man under the covers (also played by Green) threatening in song to tell a ghost story—*it is time for your spoooooky story! it's time, it's time, it's time!*—with the Green man in bed ultimately submitting and the video ending before the story is told. He also recently posted a selfie with three horrific-looking abandoned dolls that are eerily reminiscent of the Tots from *Tots TV* with the caption:

Family isn't just the best thing. It is EVERYTHING. Heck knows my little tribe (Jared 28, Chas 1, Teet also 1) can be trying at times but there's not a day that goes by where I don't thank the good lord for blessing me with these guys. Xxx #family #god #mykidsaremyworld #iddieformykids #andkill #love

Green had a small recurring part as a builder (odd odd-job man?) in the hidden-away 'black comedy-drama sitcom' *Flowers*, which I found by chance on Channel 4, maybe drawn in by Olivia Colman and Julian Barratt, a devilishly intriguing combo! Colman (the wicked stepmother in *Fleabag,* goblin queen in *The Favourite*, and goblin prey in *Peep Show*) and Barratt (the pretentious jazz toad Howard Moon in *The Mighty Boosh* and the pervy doll-loving cretin in *Killing Eve*) are Maurice and Deborah Flowers, a married couple on the brink of dissolution living in the middle of the British countryside with their adult twins.

Maurice Flowers is a depressed children's book writer whose hit is a series of books about The Grubbs, a family of goblins. He is numb to everything including his family, missing his deadlines, distressed by his live-in mother's dementia, and haunted by the disappearance of his stage magician father when he was a child. The Grubbs, we surmise, have been an outlet for him to explore his despair and sense of abandonment, and that they are clearly doppelgängers of his own family, until that is, he becomes so suicidal he finds he can no longer even write stories.

Tired of her husband hiding in his writing shed and exhausted by her deranged children, a sexually and maternally frustrated Deborah wants to smash up their whole grotto of domesticity, no longer able to wait for the day that the twins might leave the grubby nest. The twins, Donald and Amy, are both feral and frightening for different reasons. Amy's own mental health declines to the point of hallucination and the dissolution of reality—she thinks she has become a young woman from hundreds of years ago who ran away through the forest—and she repeatedly goes AWOL. She reminds me of my mum, who also lived with mental illness and would go missing on occasion when I was young, and who, like Dorothy Gale in *Return to Oz*, was institutionalised due to her poor mental health. Amy is always being screamed at by a jealous Donald who is constantly having explosive toddler-like tantrums and inventing useless contraptions, like if Caractacus Potts from *Chitty Chitty Bang Bang* had awful anger issues. Donald is played by Daniel Rigby, who won a BAFTA for playing Eric Morecambe in a double biopic of gentlemen gnomes Morecambe and Wise, narrated the *Teletubbies* reboot (Dipsey is obviously a goblin), played Bottom in *A Midsummer Night's Dream*, and is currently in a stage production of Roald Dahl's *The Witches*. Amy is played by Sophia Di Martino, who is currently playing a variant of the green God-lin of chaos Loki in the second series of *Loki*.

Flowers was written by Will Sharpe, who also plays Japanese art student Shun in the show. Shun comes to stay with this dysfunctional family so he can be the new illustrator of *The Grubbs*. (The illustrations you see in the programme are actually done by artist Staffan Gnosspelius.) *The Grubbs* books had helped

Shun get through grief after his family were all killed in a tsunami, and he is desperate for Maurice to keep *The Grubbs* going and for the Flowers family to stay together; both are the only family and home he has left. Will Sharpe recently starred in *The White Lotus* opposite a domestic-bliss-terrorist Aubrey Plaza (the mischievous and lazy April in *Parks and Recreation*, who marries accident prone gremlin Andy—they live in goblin bliss eating cereal off of Frisbees).

The intimacy and claustrophobia of domesticity are also explored in the work of the second green man, Anthony Green, an artist whose fisheye paintings draw you in with their from-above perspective, like looking into a hole in the ground and finding the Mad Hatter's tea party, though it's actually a couple in a bathroom, one of them in the bath and the other sitting on the closed toilet seat, coat hangers hovering on a washing line above them like bird skeletons. I discovered that painting, *The Bathroom at No. 29*—one of a series—as well as his celebration/commiseration of green called *My Mother Alone in Her Dining Room 74-75* in the gift shop at the Sainsbury Centre, the art gallery based at the University of East Anglia, after I had already missed the exhibition of his work. The perspective of *My Mother Alone...* is as if you're standing at the head of a dining room table with your back to a window facing the seated mother in black, whose reflection is mirrored in the unbearably shiny wooden table, behind her the room is drowning in green, a garish green carpet that looks like an aerial view of a hedge maze, similar to the one in *The Shining*, green lampshades, greenish walls, a refracted kind of watery green on the ceiling, green objects placed around the room, an ornate and gilded green cigarette box, a green marble ashtray, both ready to be touched—*OZ!*—to bring back old friends, absent family, or the dead. On the back wall is a small oval mirror which shows that no one is standing at the foot of the table at all, not Ozma, and especially not you; a trick mirror making her both alone and not alone.

There was an avocado bathroom when R and I went on a honeymoon a year after we got married. We drove around Portugal for a couple of weeks staying in hostels, an Airbnb, a B&B, but we did spend a couple of nights in a hotel as a treat. A hotel is like a stack of goblin caves, where we regress to becoming both sloth-like and re-energised teenagers, not tidying up, chucking stuff on the floor, *getting sweaty*, maybe puking from overindulgence. You couldn't get away with that at *Fawlty Towers*, the Slenderman Basil, trying so hard to raise the standards in his crumbling cave, would hunt you down. My dad migrated to the UK in 1975, the year the sitcom began, and I've always found it interesting that he, a Maltese economic migrant, found the goblinified Spanish waiter Manuel—played by an Englishman—so hilarious. The avocado bathroom at the hotel we found was incongruous with the rest of the room, it felt ominous at first, like opening a bathroom and finding a shit in the toilet or hair in the plughole (which reminds me of the scene in the remake of *The Grudge* where Sarah Michelle Gellar, best known as Buffy the slayer of vampires, feels the Grudge's hand coming out the back of her head through her hair as she's washing it. On the drive back from the cinema with my oldest friend Abby, who I don't see enough of, I had the uncanny feeling that the Grudge was in the car and I had to sleep with the light on for two weeks.) A retro, kitschy green bathroom might feel like a bad omen in a young marriage. It felt like something that might be the hinge in a short story about a melancholic and doomed trip away. I personally loved the bathroom because we had triumphed over it and its connotations—it wasn't a projection of tension and sadness in our actual marriage or a reminder of how our relationship will age and become outdated—it was just an avocado bathroom, nothing more. (Because I was googling avocado bathroom, I just got an advert from a 70s avocado kitchen set, a family of overcooked-pea-green cookware.)

In the novella *Self Portrait in Green* written by Marie NDiaye and translated by Jordan Stump, described in a review by Jennifer Brough as being filled with 'an uncanny valley of "slippery silhouettes"', green might signify many things including defiance, misbehaviour, and a shift in reality. There are a series of women in green who become the protagonist's doppelgängers in her inclusion and fixation on them and not herself, including the protagonist's mother, who Brough describes as starting a 'green-tinged life' because she left to have another family, and two green women who seemingly perish and yet return. (Author Naomi Klein writes in her book *Doppelganger: A Trip Into The Mirror World* about becoming obsessed with her Doppel, the disgraced author Naomi Wolf, who went from cultural commentator to right wing conspiracy theorist, defining the doppelgänger after Freud as something familiar that is 'suddenly alien'.) Another woman in green is the feminised river that sloshes either end of the book, perhaps the menacing green of the constantly rising threat of climate crisis. Today, as in right now, Hastings is flooded for the fifth time in three years, the shopping centre in New Town was built on a former quagmire, I technically live in a ghost bog.

I recently misread a tweet by Lucy Writers Platform editor and critic Hannah Hutchings-Georgiou where she said something about having had an essay published called "Seeing Green in The London Magazine", and mistakenly thought—or my brain took a frog hop—that it was an essay about all the mentions of the colour green in the whole history of the magazine.

I plucked, re-landscaped and replanted all the greens from her essay, about the artist Megan Barker, to quench my green thirst:

'Seeing Green in "Seeing Green"'
After Hannah Hutchings-Georgiou

seeing green
the woman in the half-state of it all fades green too
greens fade to browns to greens again

      alone in a wild wilderness of transporting greens
      this here pillow of dense green
      shrubs and soil obscure her green-clad form

the green-streaked sky
the unblemished blur of breezy greens

      magnificently fluctuating greens
      yellowing decay growing green again come spring
      forged of self and darkening green beneath

variegated palette of greens
and greens
there in the greens

this whole green and greening vision
ocular field of green and greening vision
in these green and greening visions

a green passage, a parsing green, a green that passes
in seeing green she sees
what is now green

Choosing what to read, by the way, doesn't have to be an intellectual conundrum or canonical or chronological, it can be elemental. 'A lot of reading in green this weekend', a Bookstagrammer writes under a photo of a selection of green-covered books, 'Matcha and some greenish translated fiction go together quite nicely, if not spiritually, then at least aesthetically', Dead Ink Bookshop post on X with a photo of a stack of green books and a mug filled with a pale pondy green foam; a choice as arbitrary as choosing a specific coloured object in a charity shop.

Lydia Bunt reviewed *Self Portrait in Green* during the pandemic: 'we have experienced stagnation, the sense of time repeating itself—the failure to progress beyond the same old norms, returning into lockdown time and again. NDiaye's circular narrative, lacking progressive chronology, hits close to home.' I don't think I've broken free of pandemic time, I feel locked into it, time was paused and I haven't heard the clock ticking since. Incidentally,

I'm sure someone's already writing a book about literary criticism during the pandemic, every time it's mentioned and used to frame or focus an essay, what a handy anchor it was, like saying boomers, millennials, Gen X, Gen Z. *It's not easy being Gen Z...* Kermit the Frog's song "It's Not Easy Being Green" was about how hard it is being a different colour, but is also about being proud to be different.

Green means safety, the green man at the traffic crossing, the green light, and being correct, a green tick, but also something dangerous, poisonous, toxic (though frogs are usually green, it's the not-green ones that you have to watch for). The COVID virus has been portrayed as a goblin (I also saw a poster where long COVID was depicted as Shrek), as have germs, there's one I see on a poster in a local café I frequent reminding you to wash your hands thoroughly illustrated by a gremliny, slimy, snag-toothed and green-as-hell germ, like an acid green inkblot. Looking and feeling green—as opposed to looking and feeling blue (or being yellow like the Cowardly Lion)—connotes illness, sickness, though you can also be blue and green at the same time. Being blue-green is when The Blues make you a creature: 'Have never been one to personally ascribe to Seasonal Affective Disorder but the impact January sun is having on me is mental', the writer Elise Bell wrote on X, 'literal night and day. The sun comes out and I go from goblin to beam of joy.' To be a goblin is to be lethargic, but perhaps mostly it has come to mean reclusiveness, shunning sunlight, lying around. Teenagers have been described as goblins for years due to their slovenliness and shutting themselves away in their rooms, hunched in front of magazines, books, consoles, TVs, laptops, gaming rigs, and there were others who would be called goblins pejoratively, those who never left the house, those who hoarded, those who didn't want to focus on their appearance. But suddenly, those who weren't allowed to leave the house during the pandemic, who had to stay indoors and could let their grooming slide and who found that their energy levels were dropping, those who felt somehow rebellious and naughty because they weren't being their most productive, embraced the term goblin, and *goblin mode* became the word of the year in 'post-pandemic' (that is, after-pandemic-started-happening) 2022.

When goblin mode started being used to describe this new shared experience, writers who are disabled pointed out that goblin mode had been around for a long time and couldn't solely be depicted as a lifestyle choice. Hannah Turner starts her essay "As a Disabled Woman, Goblin Mode Doesn't Sit Right With Me" describing the blink-in-the-cave-and-you'd-miss-it trajectory of how the concept of goblin mode went from its proto principles of pushing back against capitalist and perfectionist modes of being and presentation, to its adoption as simply quirkiness and mild rebellion (cue the minimising manic pixie dream girl; the photo with the article is a girl looking at her phone in front of a fridge with an open can of squirty cream in her hand), through to those 'waking up before the sun to drink green things' for me-time and those wealthy enough to escape cities for the countryside right at the start of the pandemic to live out their cottagecore fantasies.

As the pandemic went on people let go of the trappings, responsibilities and routines of society and a social life, shed moisturised skin, and went goblin. But Turner speaks of her own experience of being disabled and how it wasn't a moment of self-actualisation or a respite from life, it is her reality:

Crip communities often embody goblin mode because there is often no choice not to. I am writing this in the same outfit I have been wearing since last Sunday, my hair is over a week unwashed and, truly, I stink. I do not tell you that as a badge of honour, to prove how goblin I am. It is simply a regular occurrence in my life as a disabled person, working and living amid the often hellish landscape we are all trying to navigate.

Though there are positives to many people questioning and rebelling against the kind of perfection society dictates, Turner argues that only some people get to show themselves being goblins: '…who gets to join in? I haven't ever publicised my goblin mode, except in private groups with online disabled friends. I keep up appearances as a good, working, disabled woman on my social media, mostly to ensure I retain work as a member of the precarious gig economy.' I know my mum would not have been the poster girl for goblin mode.

It can be empowering to find a double or role model in the wild, no matter how slimy they are. Let us for a moment consider the slug, as Abi Palmer does in *Slug: A Manifesto*, which is about embracing slugness as a 'marginalised girlie': 'My brain is thick and foggy. I am soft and wet and oily'; or how about the moss-covered sloth: '[S]loth communism is the next big thing' Richard Chapman, a neurodivergent philosopher and author of *Empire of Normality: Neurodiversity and Capitalism* writes on X, 'Slovenliness, degrowth, taking the day off. The age of productivist hyper-consumption is over. We're moving into a new and peaceful age marked by a decrease in the pace of living and working. I can't wait.'

As Turner points out in her article, however, not every disabled person would want to be considered a goblin (or a slug, or a sloth) for pretty obvious reasons, such as its othering potential, but also because illness or being neurodivergent can feel like the creature you're trying to escape, like paintings depicting sleep paralysis and nightmares where a demon is sitting on the non-sleeper's chest (which has been somewhat usurped by memes of cats sitting on the chest of their owner).

Before Dorothy Gale ends the Nome King, she escapes a sanitorium where she is meant to be treated for delusions and insomnia caused by her first escapade in Oz. She ends up back in Oz where she has to fight Wheelers (like '77 punks with squeaky wheels instead of feet) and Princess Mombi (who can take her head off and replace it with the stolen heads of women she keeps in a room of glass display cases). The film's director, Walter Murch, was shocked and hurt that people found the film so petrifying, and the backlash basically ruined his career as a film director. In one interview he says that he believes one reason people found it so frightening is that it's not a musical—there aren't any jolly songs to break the terror. A second reason is because Dorothy is actually played by a young girl—an eleven-year-old Fairuza Balk, who would go on to star in *The Craft*. Yet another reason Murch thinks the film scared people is that Aunt Em, the mother figure in the film, doesn't get mother's intuition and take Dorothy home immediately from the creepy sanitorium where she takes Dorothy for 'electric healing' for her insomnia ('you're no help to me in the morning') and hallucinations. Why doesn't Aunt Em twig that something super sinister is going on? Doesn't she care? Nothing's scarier than a bad mother. But what if the bad mother had been institutionalised and given experimental therapies as a girl, like my mum?

In her memoir *Gargoyles*, Harriet Mercer writes of having a health crisis that makes her see demonic gargoyles in a waking nightmare that lasts the six weeks she is in hospital, forcing her to think about what in her life and her subconscious has spawned these creatures—the gargoyle both a metaphor of unexplored trauma and of illness itself. (My friend Tommy introduced me to the cartoon *Gargoyles*, which I couldn't get into, apparently Kenneth Branagh, a terrible Poirot, the soft Belgian gnome, is making it into a live-action film.) Some have embraced the term goblin and its many variants. In *Golem Girl*, artist and writer Riva Lehrer explores three questions: 'What do we sacrifice in the pursuit of normalcy? What becomes possible when we embrace monstrosity? Can we envision a world that [only] sees impossible creatures?' Lehrer's writing and art practice are focused on the 'socially challenged body' conjuring the Social Model of Disability; one is not disabled in themselves, that is, by their body, identity or mind, but rather by an inflexible, uncaring and unsupportive society that shuns people with impairments. Lehrer has to remake herself and be remade to live in the world: 'Lehrer often describes feeling like a golem, which, according to Jewish folklore, is an anthropomorphic, man-made creature, typically made out of clay or soil, magically brought to life. Through all of the dozens of surgeries that Lehrer endures, over time her body becomes so altered that she views herself as golem-like.' Often the only characters that seem to fit with these experiences in storytelling are monsters. Embracing the monster means being seen, even through a green lens. In *Disfigured: On Fairy Tales, Disability, and Making Space*, Amanda Leduc explores the ways disabled people have been goblinised in folk tales, asking 'so what happens when you identify more with the Beast than Beauty?' and 'if every disabled character is mocked and mistreated, how does the Beast ever imagine a happily-ever-after?' There are countless examples of ableism in film where disabled people are portrayed as psychotic murderers (the killer in *Don't Look Now*, played by Adelina Poerio), non-human creatures (the munchkins in *The Wizard of Oz*), or superhuman (Ruben the oracle in *Midsommar*); or characters with learning disabilities, dementia-like illnesses or head trauma are seen as dangerous and/or worthy of ridicule (imprisoned Sloth in *The Goonies*, Arthur who has had a brain injury in *Joker*, the 'devolved' Goombas in *Super Mario Bros.*, lobotomised Zeno in *Altes Geld*, the grandmother in *Don't Hug Me I'm Scared*); or characters with mental illnesses (too many to count). In each case, there is dehumanisation and infantilisation, accompanied by the manipulation of the viewer to feel fearful or superior.

Artists in general seek solitude, we think of the writer tucked away in archives or nooks, outside of the thrum of society—it can give the impression that they think they're above regular humans. 'Obviously periods of seclusion are really useful when writing long works of prose and I do it when I'm able and it's necessary', the author Shola von Reinhold says in an interview, 'but the implication that it's somehow ennobling is putrid to me!' Then there are those who are in exile—forced or self-chosen because it felt like the only way, beyond cottagecore and into hermitage. Like Quasimodo in the bell tower in *The Hunchback of Notre Dame*. Like Joni Mitchell, who sought self-described hermitude after criticism alienated her from music-making, or John Mulaney going to rehab for drug addiction as described in his stand-up show *Baby J*, or like in the memoir *Hermit*, where Jade "Green" Angeles Fitton writes about the underexplored figure of the woman hermit and living alone in nature after being left by her abusive partner. A woman hermit might be given another name, a hag—a woman deemed outside of society, made invisible through aging, sometimes interchangeable with the figure of the witch—*night hag* is also another name for the sleep paralysis demon.

In her novel *Circe*, Madeleine Miller's retelling of the Circe tale, the titular minor goddess, often portrayed as a villain, is banished to an island for witchcraft (she turned a love rival into a monster), where she must battle away men who come ashore, suffering greatly at their hands. We could imagine Circe as a sister to Medusa in Greek-myth-hag exile. Medusa, who has a nest of hissing snakes for hair, could be considered an exiled 'hag', a woman monster we were told to fear because she turns men to stone on an island of Gorgons. (In D. H. Lawrence's incredible poem "Snake" about a man who finds a poisonous snake drinking from his water trough and then watches it slither through a hole in the wall, the snake is seen as an exiled king; in Wes Anderson's short film *Poison*, based on a Roald Dahl short story, Dev Patel and Ben Kingsley save Benedict Cumberbatch from a poisonous snake, only for him to come out with a racist outburst— in Alfred Hitchcock's previous adaptation this eruption is mellowed by the mysterious snake's prisoner Pope being an alcoholic, in Anderson's version, Pope is just an ungrateful racist with a fragile ego, as toxic as the venomous snake.) What you don't often get told is that Medusa was turned into a Gorgon as punishment for being raped by Poseidon, and that she kills men with a stony look for her own protection—she is nothing more than a conquest to them.

In any case, Meg Mucklebones from *Legend* is Medusa's doppelgänger, they too could be sisters. Both green-grey sisters are killed by men with shields. Perseus uses his to navigate his way closer and closer to Medusa without her stony gaze hitting him, while Meg is distracted by her reflection in Jack's shield as he flatters her (why is she so susceptible to flattery if not because she is unloved, a kind of "spinster"?) and in both cases their heads are cut off. Instead of Medusa's gargoyle-grey skin, Meg has goblin-green skin, like the green witch in *The Wizard of Oz* (green witches often look like goblins in robes and hats, or goblins look like naked witches). Witches always have those twitchy witchy hands, all green-fingered.

House plants are the proliferation of goblins in the home (and not just the cannibalistic plant in *The Little Shop of Horrors*), they make us green-fingered too. R is the gardener, he pots and feeds and waters these creatures all over our house, spider plants hanging down from shelves like witch's hands, cacti all squat and spiky like poisonous toads. If I'm always looking for green objects in junk shops, R's always looking for plant containers. While he's trying to find something practical to repot his green pets like hermit crabs moving from home to home ('I love hermit crabs, they're like nature's goblins', someone wrote on Instagram, alongside a video of a hermit crab that had moved into a clear glass jar, 'TW: crab butt'), I'm off searching for the green glow of something.

I was in a charity shop in my hometown Shoreham-by-Sea with my dad, my brother and my sister-in-law during our first Christmas post-Mum (that is, post-mourning-beginning) a few months ago, and there was a lot of distracting green: Christmas trees, holly, elf outfits. (Pee-wee Herman, whose alter-ego played

Pinocchio in Shelley Duvall's *Faerie Tale Theatre*, is the player of vengeful tricks, 'a bratty precocious kid... controlled by the incubus—the manifestation of evil itself' as *Bad Santa*-esque David Letterman described him, is elven all year round in his Playhouse, his zippy grotto full of friends, but especially during the Christmas episode, where goblinific Grace Jones dances hypnotically and Cher screams—have you seen Grace Jones slurping oysters with Alan Carr on his old chat show?) My dad told us all to pick something out and he would get it for us as our Christmas present—a hoody for my sister-in-law, a jumper for R in his absence, a T-shirt for my brother, and I chose a meadow-green raincoat, like a detective coat really, something Columbo could wear to a wedding or Jack in the Green, definitely not rainproof, barely even splashproof, but bright green nonetheless. I started a list on my phone a while ago called "Colours You Look Good In" to remind myself what colours to wear that compliment my olive (olive!) skin, dark brown hair, dark brown eyes, and actually I knew that I look way better in mint green, so I undermined myself, tricked myself. This coat would look good on someone with red hair (think Ariel in *The Little Mermaid*, her bright red hair, her shimmering green tail). There was a huge backlash against the green coat worn by the red-haired Nicole Kidman in the very boring-seeming show *The Undoing*.

either an exemplar of boho-chic or a vestige of Middle Earth, depending on personal taste.

—Vogue

Sludge-green [...] The ugly green coat in the HBO drama *The Undoing* has usurped a starry cast [...] this coat is worn again and again by Nicole Kidman's character, a gnomic therapist.
—Guardian

I wanted to do something that was a cinematic coat, something that you would remember [...] I wanted her to be able to have a coat that was almost kind of a shield. I wanted her also to kind of feel that she could disappear in it.
—*Signe Sejlund, costume designer,* Harpers Bazaar

'Gnomic' isn't usually used to describe a person, it's used to describe an enigmatic or ambiguous remark and a 'gnome' is a wise saying or aphorism. But I'm not the grammar police, and I think words can handle taking on more meaning. As Jake Peralta, the hyperactive manchild detective, eloquently says in *Brooklyn 99*, 'stuff can be two things.' I wore my green coat once and it made me sweaty and slimy. I think the coat in *The Undoing* makes Kidman look like an iguana. Fun fact: Jennifer Lopez's notorious snaky green Versace dress was the reason that Google Image Search was invented. So many people went on a search/quest for this dress that they had to invent new technology. (Because I was googling green dresses, I got an advert of a bored woman swanning around in west London in a 'casual'/casually ugly green dress.) Another fun fact: the prototype for Kermit the Frog was made from Jim Henson's mother's green coat. (Puppeteer Wendy Froud, who worked numerous times with Henson including creating the goblins of *Labyrinth* with her husband Brian and the Podlings, Gelflings, 'sleazy, snakey'—the puppeteer's words—Skeksis and Mystics of *The Dark Crystal*, is best known for fabricating the prototype for Yoda—she is known as 'the mother of Yoda' [she's the actual mother of baby Toby in *Labyrinth*] though she isn't well known. I've just realised that *The Mandalorian* is like *Three Men and a Baby* but in space—*The Mandalorian and a Baby Yoda*.) Everyone's still talking about the green silk dress Keira Knightley wears as Cecilia in *Atonement*. The greenest, silkiest most enchanting frog-green kind of dress, which she's wearing when she has sex with James McAvoy's Robbie in the library as part of a hot summer/upstairs-downstairs *Lady Chatterley's Lover/The Go-Between* kind of situation. Cecilia's younger sister Briony, played by Saoirse Ronan, sneakily spies on their illicit rendezvous and this sight, paired with the erotic letter she *opens and reads* instead of delivering from Robbie/James to Cecilia/Keira, leads her to conclude that Robbie is a sex pest and must be the rapist she sees attacking her friend Lola/Juno Temple in the dark grounds of the house rather than Paul/Benedict Cumberbatch. Her decision to point the green finger at Robbie has many horrific consequences: he is sent to fight in the war, Robbie and Cecilia can never be properly together again, Robbie is brutalised by PTSD, and he eventually dies of sepsis on the beach before making it back home. There's a photo that tickles me green of Jodie Comer of *Killing Eve* in a green dress with puffy sleeves at an award's show where she's not standing straight and demure; she's hunched and froggy, making a mischievous screwed-up face, sticking out her tongue, and wrestling with fellow actor Andrew Scott in a mushroom-white suit over a Golden Globe. *Scott* rhymes with *hot*. Is the Hot Priest in *Fleabag* a goblin? Would there have been a future for *Fleabag* the Goblinette and her sinning vicar? As likely as Eve Polastri and Villanelle. Awards in general are slimy illusions of meritocracy (I would say that in my bitter green, non-award-winning voice). They're subjective (personal taste of an assembly of judges), they've proven to be nepotistic (judges voting for friends, colleagues, people with the same publisher), they're exclusionary (certain forms of writing aren't accepted, writers of a certain age aren't eligible even though many groups of writers take longer to get published, plus publishers often have to submit a pile of books at personal cost and sometimes even have to pay for award promotion if their book is nominated). If I won an award, would I be happy and covetous of it? *YES!* But then, a new shame would creep in—the shame of being validated by an institution, for validating prize culture. But to be honest I need the exposure and importantly the money, and I'm apparently too old (at 37) to be allowed to apply to a swathe of funding. I need that green. (Jim Henson had a shrine to money in his puppeteering workshop.) I have been known to become green with envy, and I can remember all the times I became the green-eyed monster, because it was always followed by a deep shame. *I am not usually like this!* And perhaps envy isn't followed by shame, but is actually shame, a sense of deep embarrassment at having not achieved something. When in a jealous state you think 'why not me, why didn't I get it'. But it's a false idea. It was never yours, not for a moment. You never owned it, it can't be stolen. A novel I wrote didn't get nominated for awards, but I actually didn't mind, I had no expectations. It was only when a writer I admired got in touch to say that they thought that my lack of recognition from a certain prize was an 'omission' that I got upset. It made me picture a display of books face out on the shelf, and a gap where my book should have been, *had been until...* it made it an active thing, rather than a passive thing. But this image is a mirage. I have a Post-it on my computer that reads *envy is the thief of joy*. It's the green-tinted spectacles that filter your life.

The closest thing I have to an award and the only object I consider a close match to my coveted green ornament is a vase in our home by our friend and old flatmate Sophie (we lived alongside seven others in a warehouse, half of us unknown to the landlord), that I had admired from afar and which she gave to R for his birthday. The vase looks like a trophy with two wiggly handles and is a deep magical green. I've still not found the perfect green object that shimmers at the back of my mind though, one that might somehow be a portal to lead me back to those long-lost friends who've petrified in time and who I can't seem to find. Maybe I should stop looking for the perfect green object. The green vase reminds me that if I reach out, say *HI!*, I can be reunited with friends still within my grasp. I just have to take a risk, seek them out. There are more than three attempts, but if you don't use them...

I just walked past a shop window display for the Jack in the Green festival, which is happening this weekend. Of the dozens of green objects in the window, not a single one was perfect. I continue to wait for a sign from the universe that I should return to the world, to life.

GREENSWARD

I manifest at the front of a procession
a towering tree-man with a rigid green face
ribbons streaming from him like fireworks
leads us on a merry dance
there are mushroom-women, toad-girls
giant milkmaids and horned beasts
bells hiss on my wrists and ankles
the treeman twirls and staggers and sings

Fleck of green!
Fleck of green!
A froglet fleck of green
Just for me, just for me
A froglet fleck of green
Fleck of green!
Fleck of green!

I have forgotten the dance, the banners
bear unfamiliar names and causes, the drums are out of sync
we're marching up the hill, up to the castle
long ruined, to carry out a sacrifice
hands pull and push me, I jangle like keys
I see the castle rebuilt on the hill
a citadel, its residents peering down at me from the
battlements, laughing. I look down and I'm flocked with leaves
the greenwoman to be plucked by the crowd

my bells toll and tell on me as I start running
they turn into bumblebees and buzz off
my greenery blows down the slope
I roll away after it, shouts tumble after me.

GURN

ON PUPPETS AND PUPPET MASTERS

My week only truly begins when the X account @wejustnormalmen posts the same 45-second video every Monday like clockwork.

A camera is zoomed in on a woman with shoulder-length dark hair and deep red lipstick face to face with a puppet dog.

The puppet says: "We're just normal men."

The woman is holding back a laugh, twice or thrice her shoulders involuntarily hunch forward, she keeps pressing her lips shut. The camera starts to slowly pan out. We see the woman is wearing a white shirt with a black feathery motif, the dog puppet is in a garishly colourful shirt.

The woman and dog look towards the camera, her seemingly unsure of what's going on, the dog mirroring her. They both look back at one another, and the woman asks: "What do you mean 'normal men'?"

Then the dog says: "We're just innocent men."

The woman's held back laugh snorts in her throat and nose, she raises her hand to her mouth, a move-it-along song starts playing. It's all over in eight seconds, though the video continues as she presses her eyes shut, her mouth in a grin, her shoulders shaking; she never recovers.

Liking this video every Monday morning is like ticking an item off my to-do list, it's practically part of my job. It makes me laugh every time; laughter is the music that plays to boot me up. This video of a young woman laughing in dark red lipstick (I tried

to find this colour everywhere, I don't know why exactly, perhaps
I thought it contained that snorting laugh, maybe it's magical, or
maybe slippery colour-theory means I will never be able to find the
right shade), giggling with her puppet mate who's aping her body
language as the camera pulls back, is just perfect somehow. There's
an article called "A Forensic Investigation into Why the 'we're just
normal men' Meme Fills Us With Such Joy" on Planet Woo where
the two meme-stars are interviewed. Hacker T. Dog puppeteer
Phil Fletcher explains the backstory, subject of much conspiracy,
that instead of keeping to script between shows on CBBC, he said
something at random to presenter Lauren Layfield, making her
corpse—sorry, I mean, it's not Fletcher that makes her corpse, it's
Hacker T. Dog. 'Phil [sic? Hacker] is a tyrant and loves to make
you laugh', Layfield says in the article, and when asked about the
popularity of the meme, Fletcher-Hacker says that 'It's just an idiot
talking rubbish to another idiot.'

    Let's just get straight into it: all puppets are goblins.
My first real exposure to both puppets and goblins was *Labyrinth*.
I learned the alphabet and basically how to speak from *Sesame
Street*, and yes, many puppets in *Sesame Street* (and *Fraggle Rock*,
and *The Muppet Show* – Muppet = marionette + puppet) are cute
in appearance, but there's also the Grouch (green, lives in a *trash can*
and his best friend is a worm called Slimy, his cousin is probably the
Grinch, Jim Carey's other green-faced imp; Alice Munro describes
putting off a story that's going badly as 'grouching around'—Munro's
legacy has become rotten trash since it came to light that she
failed to act on her husband Gerald Fremlin abusing her daughter
when she was a child, *Fremlin rhymes with...*), the Cookie Monster

(who gorges on cookies, like that feckless scrounger Mandy in *Mandy*, written and starring Diane Morgan, best known as history-programme-gremlin Philomena Cunk; Mandy gets her dream job at a biscuit factory, but soon becomes sick of eating biscuits, rushing to be sick in a stairwell only to fall down multiple flights of stairs in her biscuit-induced daze), Bert (he gives us all permission to be introverted and grumpy and mysterious), Kermit (he's a frog, though he wasn't always, he started by just being thought of as 'the little green guy'; Fozzy: 'Listen, you meet a frog without a sense of humour, you're looking at a green lump'), Miss Piggy (she's a pig; remember when the parents get turned into pigs in *Spirited Away* because they're more interested in food than their child?), Rizzo the Rat (he's a rat; at the time of writing it's a 'hot rodent boyfriend summer' apparently, according to listicles Jeremy Allen White from *The Bear* is attractive due to being rat-like, though you probably won't find Ralph Fiennes attractive as a rattish, 'lean and leathery' ratter with a voice that has the 'soft throaty sound of a croaking frog' in *The Rat Catcher*—a short film by Wes Anderson based on a Roald Dahl story that feels like a modern-day *The Storyteller* episode and who freaks out Richard Ayoade—basement-dweller Maurice "Mossy" Moss in *The I.T. Crowd*—and Rupert Friend by biting the head off a rat for a bet) and Animal (wild, and a drummer). There are so many puppet goblins: Badger from *Bodger and Badger*, Emu who attacked Parkinson, green Orvil in his nappy, Gordon the Gopher, Zippy from *Rainbow*, Sweep from *Sooty and Sweep*. Otis the Aardvark once made a song and dance about pronouncing my last name when a photo I sent in to CBBC got featured, which was either hilarious or embarrassing, I can't remember, I was about nine or ten I think. Everyone at school seemed to have a Sooty or Sweep (never Sue) puppet. The best kind of puppet a kid could have was obviously a Boglin, covered in jellyflesh on the outside (which would pick up dust in its stickiness, similar to those aliens in eggs—I had one go mouldy inside its shell). The writer Richard V. Hirst, who once commissioned me to write a short story for an anthology inspired by David Bowie's album *Low*, posted a home video of him as a child with a Boglin on his hand, which he's making chatter away enthusiastically, at odds with the shy-looking boy controlling him. Elmo went viral recently because he posted from the *Sesame Street* X account simply asking, 'How is everybody doing?' People didn't hold back, he opened the floodgates. Mr. Frond, the school guidance councillor in *Bob's Burgers*, has various dolls and puppets he uses to get children to talk about their feelings. I recently saw a video of a young Palestinian girl who could only talk about the murder of her father by Israeli forces to her hand puppet. In the recent Jim Henson documentary *Jim Henson: Idea Man*, it's stated that puppets can say things we want to say, or what we wished our parents would say/had said. A puppet creates a safety barrier for the sharing of emotions or frustrations. Kendra, who Tina babysits one time in *Bob's Burgers*, makes her teddy bear speak with a 'gremlin' voice and enjoys expressing herself by kicking people in the crotch. Bob himself makes slabs of meat and Thanksgiving turkeys talk, he turns them into meat puppets so he can chat with them when he's alone.

Whether the puppet is adorable or not, it's not all about appearance and character. Puppets are goblins because they are just fundamentally unpredictable, the vessels for mischief, and twitchy as spiders. Puppets are also being controlled by some other energy, some other force. The puppet master controls things in the dark. Tom Böttcher, a young German actor I follow on Instagram, who's starting to get his big break (he recently played Pip the Jester in a made-for-TV Märchen [fairy tale] and has a baddie part in a German Netflix thriller) is the puppet and the puppet master simultaneously. He posts videos where he performs as a marionette, like a living Thunderbird, and miraculously, when the camera cuts to his feet, he is stepping through the air, both feet off the ground. These marionette videos are very popular, but one of his most popular videos is him pretending to be a NPC, a non-player character; one of those figures you can engage with in a computer game, like a seller or a guard, but can't play as. I found this too creepy though, I only rewatch the marionette videos. (Two memoirists I know have an interest in marionettes: Doireann Ní Ghríofa has instructions of how to make a paper marionette in her memoir *A Ghost in the Throat*, the marionette being a paper version of both the writer she is researching and herself, and Noreen Masud, author of the memoir *A Flat Place*, posted online about making marionettes out of bones—this feels like an apt metaphor for what memoir is.) Böttcher is very sweet and seems to be growing into one of those guys who could get a real following. He can play impish and naïve, but also villainous. He reminds me a bit of Joseph Quinn who plays Eddie Munson in *Stranger Things*. Boy, that wig is the real star! Fans completely lost their minds over that character. They even started trolling the actress who is his barely-a-love-interest in the show. He's a poor man's (no, let's scrap the classist crap actually) rip-off/ bootleg version of Heath Ledger's Patrick in *10 Things I Hate About You*. Every character in *Stranger Things* has been seen before, they're all doppelgängers from past 80s films and TV shows, like they're AI generated, like it's an extra-long version of the deranged sitcom spoof video *Too Many Cooks*. *Don't Hug Me I'm Scared*, the dark puppet show, also reminds you of every children's show from the 80s/90s—the Red one is like a long Elmo, the Duck is the duck with the long mournful quack from *Rosie and Jim*'s houseboat but with an attitude problem, the Yellow One is like Ernie, Todney and Lily are the Tiny Tots, the house is... every house in a children's show. When I had COVID one hot July week, I put out our shit sofa bed with the blinds closed and rewatched cool-and-dark vibed *Labyrinth* and then the finale episode (it's really a film) of *Stranger Things* season 3. I noticed for the first time that Vecna is the Goblin King to Eleven's Sarah. I noticed that the chiming clock in the Upside Down has the same sound effect as the chiming clock in *Labyrinth*. It was disconcerting as an 80s' kid, but I realise that a kid born in '08 doesn't know they're watching an amalgamation or an echo of my whole childhood. *10 Things I Hate About You* is an amalgamation of Shakespeare's *The Taming of the Shrew* and a million high school movies. Heath Ledger's character, and Joseph Quinn's character, are James Dean, etc. Do 'oos kids need to know the references? It sounds too much like the moan of Metallica fans that got annoyed that a whole new generation came to the band through *Stranger Things*.

Böttcher reminds me of the automaton scene in the castle in the fictional Germanic state of Vulgaria in *Chitty Chitty Bang Bang* (filmed in Germany of course—you can see a Rathaus [town hall], a Hotel Einhorn [Hotel Unicorn], a hanging shop sign of a pretzel. Vulgaria sounds like a drag name, it probably has been), where Dick

Van Dyke's Caractacus Potts and sweet heiress Truly Scrumptious play a stringless marionette and a wind-up dancer respectively. Böttcher's marionette movements in his videos are so innocent, he embodies the puppet-self as blank canvas, voiceless. Gollum, though embodied by Andy Serkis, is the opposite. Gollum is basically a puppet sewn together with pixels. He's a puppet not with Andy Serkis' hand up it and Serkis' voice, but with the whole of Andy Serkis inside it wearing tight green spandex! The spandex was actually blue or purple or white, but often is green for use with the green screen, the magical cloak to wear in the enchanted forest. The enchanted forest in *Legend* looks like an AI-created nightmare even though it was the 80s. There's an Instagram account called @sentientmuppetfactory where an artist creates disturbing Muppet-esque characters using AI that look like humans and puppets painfully fused together. In a Guardian interview with Peter Friedman who plays Frank in *Succession,* one of the media lords in a tower on the edge of the maze of New York, it's not only brought up that his character is compared to a well-known Muppet, but that he was also at one point a puppeteer on the Muppets.

Frank and Karl have been compared to Statler and Waldorf. Weren't you a Muppeteer in the late 70s?
Yes. I've done right hands for a lot of famous puppets. I never touched those guys but I can see the resemblance.

Weren't you also Mr Snuffleupagus on *Sesame Street?*
Only half of him. I was the back end, the business end, although you have the easier gig because you're not doing the mouth movements

to Jerry Nelson's voiceover. It's sweaty work inside Snuffy but as a 28-year-old making $50 per shot, it was all worth it.

Personally, I think that it's Frank (Peter Friedman) and Hugo (Fisher Stevens) who are like the grumbling old snob puppets. Karl (David Rasche) is more like Sam Eagle. Brian Cox's patriarch Logan Roy is like both balcony-dwelling hecklers rolled into one.

There's a great episode of *Columbo* starring Fisher Stevens called "Murder, Smoke and Shadows" that I watched at my parents' house. Stevens' character is being blackmailed over a video that shows that while making a student film, he left a young woman to die during the filming of a stunt. When her ex-boyfriend finds the film years later, after Stevens' character has become a big film producer, he tries to blackmail him, and ends up getting killed by Fisher through electrocution on a filmset. Stevens' character tries to convince the ex-boyfriend that this unintentional snuff film is fake at first. It reminded me of one of my favourite films, *Blow Up*, where a photographer loses his mind trying to figure out if one of his photos shows a dead body in a park. He zooms in closer and closer using an analogue method in a dark room, but the photo just becomes more and more pixelated, more and more abstract, until it just looks mottled, like cold, grey, dead flesh. Photo and film veracity is getting harder and harder now, photoshop, deepfakes; once considered the mediums of truth and proof, this is no longer the case, though they never really showed the truth, they've always been a goblin in a suit given the benefit of the doubt. Robin Williams plays a man impersonating a cop in an episode of *Law and Order: Special Victims Unit* who has a record for 'mischief' and who represents himself in court—he convinces the jury that a photo of him at the scene of the crime should be dismissed because investigators used an algorithm to make it clearer.

There's a meta moment in the reveal part of the *Columbo* episode that makes you disbelieve your eyes. Columbo, in an uncharacteristically surreal flourish, is momentarily transformed into a circus ringmaster. (I think of Graham Norton, our greatest interviewer, as a ringmaster for the greatest show on earth, with his sparkly and embroidered jackets. He makes his guests jig and play the fool under his spell.)

Before you know it (I had to rewind it), there's a flash of Columbo in his brown Mac, a flash of dumbstruck Fisher Stevens, a flash of red coat-tail-wearing and bowing Columbo. He brings on detectives playing waiters—actually, actors playing detectives acting as waiters—for their curtain call. Fisher Stevens had been played!

Fisher Stevens was in *Short Circuit*, where the grasshopper-like military robot Johnny 5 gains consciousness, starts mimicking the gurning japes of *The Three Stooges* and goes on chaotic, messy rampages. We would watch *Short Circuit* constantly as children, usually followed by *Batteries Not Included* and *Flight of the Navigator* (Max is voiced by Paul Reubens, a.k.a. Pee-wee Herman), where mischievous and magical imps were replaced by mischievous and magical robots. As the 80s turned into the 90s and the 00s and the 10s, people who hadn't ever had to worry about racism before noticed after countless reruns (and a sequel) that Fisher Stevens, who identifies as white Jewish, had been doing brownface as an Indian man to play Ben Jabituya. When you're a kid in the 80s you don't necessarily pick up on nuance like this, but you spot it now, on a Sunday rerun, like someone put a frame of a goblin flashing up on the screen. Behind the cartoon mask of Apu, Carl, and Bumblebee Man in *The Simpsons* was Hank Azaria doing a goblinifying impression all along. In *Chitty Chitty Bang Bang*, the kind toymaker (played by Benny Hill, forever chasing girls around bushes to wacky music) has a golliwog displayed in his toyshop. In *The Red Shoes*, which I also recently saw, there's a flash of blackface, which I googled afterwards and had verified on a few movie blogs. The Child Catcher in *Chitty Chitty Bang Bang* is reminiscent of Nazi soldiers searching for Jewish people. Children are verboten in Vulgaria. They hide as jack-in-the-box puppets right under the noses of the castle guards. The Child Catcher is a long-nosed fiend (very different to Gonzo) and has been considered—partly for his caricatured appearance and partly because he's simultaneously cast as a Gestapo-y demon in black—as being antisemitic. *Chitty Chitty Bang Bang* was based on a book by Ian Fleming, the writer of James Bond (haven't got space to go into how much of a goblin Bond is), supported by one of the Bond films' producers Albert R. Broccoli (broccoli! The green nemesis of young children's dinnertime!), but the character of the Child Catcher was said to be added to the screenplay by Roald Dahl, who was openly an antisemite—John Lithgow, who played a lanky alien in *Third Rock From the Sun*, is currently performing as Dahl in a play called *Giant* about his antisemitism. Ralph Fiennes pops up as Dahl in his writing chair in a series of short films based on stories by Dahl by Wes Anderson that grapple somewhat with the legacy of Dahl's bigotry. Dahl co-wrote the screenplay with Ken Hughes and was rumoured to dislike children, so the Child Catcher must have been very enjoyable for him to scratch out in his 'curmudgeon's cave', as his writing nook is referred to in one profile.

Bradley Cooper's use of a fake nose in *Maestro* about the composer/conductor/puppet master Leonard Bernstein was accused by many of being antisemitic. Marjorie Ingall does a helpful and humorous blow-by-blow (eh, eh) in Vox which starts with 'Bradley Cooper's prosthetic schnoz—the honking appendage', before progressing to non-Jewish actors playing Jewish people, Jewface, and Jewish representation in Hollywood. While we watched the film, R said that Bradley Cooper as older Bernstein in *Maestro* looks like Hoggle from *Labyrinth*, and this is true, due to his wrinkly, leathery fake skin, and the prominent nose, which is much larger than Bernstein's real nose, it's so much a fake nose, like fake-glasses-and-fake-nose fake. It is both highly realistic and highly caricatured, it's the definition of uncanny. He also looks like all old men where their ears and noses have grown, he reminds me of my grandad, he reminds me of the BFG. Though this is a passing parallel, there is obviously a well-explored and well-documented link between the depiction of goblins and the antisemitic depictions of Jewish people. The contemporary figure of the goblin is not all that ancient, and apparently arose around the same time as growing antisemitism in Europe. There are comparative studies in Nazi propaganda depicting caricatures of Jewish people and the depiction of goblins, sometimes with complete crossover where goblins or malevolent characters are described or heavily insinuated as being Jewish in the weaponisation of fairy tales to promote antisemitism—there's numerous examples from Nazi schoolbooks, including where Jewish people are compared to an anthropomorphic poisonous toadstool hiding in the midst of other mushrooms. This isn't something that only happened during the Nazi era. The well-known poem "Goblin Market", written in 1859 by Christina Rossetti, has been read as an antisemitic 'cautionary tale'. Many fairy tales as we know them had their very beginnings as nationalistic propaganda due to the Brothers Grimm, who pulled the strings on the tales they gathered, curating/creating a specific kind of Germanness. Another perhaps surprising interpretation of "Goblin Market" is that it's about the growth of capitalism, which for some reason makes me think of *The Crystal Maze*. *The Crystal Maze* with its maze-master/labyrinth-master Richard O'Brien or Richard Ayoade (pick your Dick), and *Labyrinth* are similar not only by design but also through the challenges, the disorientation, and its charismatic and camp guide. Like *Labyrinth*, "Goblin Market" could be about losing your sexual innocence, but like *The Crystal Maze*, where you hand in your magical crystals for lots of cash, it can also be about joining 'the market', as well as queer sex, proto-feminism, or antisemitic fearmongering. Many organisations and individuals came to Cooper's defence regarding the nose and what it represented, including Bernstein's own children, now elderly, who completely disagreed with this backlash against Cooper. *Honk honk*. I picture Bernstein's kids like the grown-up Tootles in *Hook,* who is eighty-something but still full of childish mischief. When the film *Tár* came out, featuring Lydia Tár, a fictional composer/conductor/puppet master played by an ice-queening Cate Blanchett who is supposed to have studied under Leonard Bernstein, Bernstein's kids released a statement confirming her mentorship with their father, trolling the film's director who obviously poured cold water on the theory!

Tár, in my passionate opinion, is a brilliant film. I watched it twice in one week, once with my friend Kat, and once with R. This was a risk because I had done this before with dire consequences, where I had loved *Phantom Thread* so much I took R to see it a couple of days after I'd watched it alone, and he hated Daniel Day Lewis' crabby Reynolds Woodcock. But *Tár* he loved too. *Maestro* in my disappointed opinion is a terrible film. In fact, it's not really a film at all. In the review of *Maestro* in Polygon, the reviewer identifies, hitting the nail on the head, that 'it's not about a man but about a man acting'. The film is too on the nose. You can see right through the prosthetics to the goblin hungry for an Oscar beneath. *Tár* is about a woman composer who will seemingly do anything to reach the highest echelons of composing and conducting. When rumours start to float that she has been seducing her mentees as part of a programme to support young women into conducting, her tower and reign start to fall and falter. She is a bully, she cheats on her wife who is first violin (but second fiddle) in the Berlin orchestra she presides over. Once her downfall fully manifests, we learn to understand that she has gone from soft Linda Tár from a working-class immigrant family (tarred a class traitor with a look from her brother) who loved to watch Leonard Bernstein on VHS as a child, to the terrifying Lydia, a masker and mimicker of the upper-class male musician's playbook—every bum note of it. There's an infamous scene where she threatens a little girl for bullying her daughter— "Ich bin der Vater von Petra" she says, "I am Petra's father" (some people think she says "die Vater", *die* the form of 'the' that usually precedes a feminine word, therefore a kind of feminised father). Lydia is like a child catcher that's breached the gates of the playground. Robert Helpmann, who played the Child Catcher in *Chitty Chitty Bang Bang*, would apparently protect the child actors from the temper and swearing of writer and director Hughes on set. Helpmann starred in *The Red Shoes* as both the choreographer— a kind of puppet master—and the Shoemaker—who makes Moira Shearer's Victoria Page into a puppet. *The Red Shoes* is about Page, a budding ballerina, and Julian Craster, a composing student so good his professor plagiarises him, who are both discovered by charming but dastardly ballet director Lermontov. Should Lermontov's prima ballerina fall in love with anyone or anything other than ballet, he throws them out the company. He vows to make Page a star, but Craster and Page begin a not-so-secret love affair right under his nose. Both Lermontov and Craster demand Victoria Page make a choice—ballet or love. Craster actually wants her love to support his career and Lermontov just wants to own her, causing her to lose her mind and end her life; the red shoes dancing her in front of a train. Lermontov and Craster are two sides of the same puppet master coin. Like Tár, Page suffers for being a woman artist trapped among the standards of men, of art tainted by masculine control. (I would like to see *The Red Shoes* with a Black Sabbath soundtrack, the Birmingham Ballet recently used Black Sabbath's music; Ozzy Osbourne of Oz could play the Shoemaker.) A day after rewatching *The Red Shoes* at an anniversary screening at a local independent cinema in Hastings, I read Andrea Brady's memoir-essay about watching the *The Red Shoes* in the days after having had an abortion, where she cites a poem by Holly Pester called "Comic Timing" in which 'the speaker goes to Ilford, has an abortion, takes a cab home, hosts a house party and clowns around'. We can imagine them dancing around freely, because, as Brady puts it, this assertion of agency is not a tragedy as abortion is depicted as a 'farce'; 'a comedy of errors that doesn't end in a bedding, but begins with one.'

The Red Shoes, *Tár*, and *Maestro*, all have central figures—Lermontov/Craster, Lydia Tár, and Leonard Bernstein—that are doppelgängers for the Goblin King in *Labyrinth*, gobliny in their selfish, manipulative, ambitious, controlling nature, and are all in a way a cautionary tale for believing that becoming a great artist is worth the torturing of yourself and everyone around you. This is explored elsewhere in *Phantom Thread*, *Whiplash*, *The Banshees of Inisherin*. A theory was going around that *The Banshees of Inisherin* is inspired by the books *Frog and Toad*, and someone made a wicked-good mini video game of it. Reece Shearsmith and Steve Pemberton, the double act behind *Inside No. 9* and *The League of Gentlemen* strike me as a *Frog and Toad*—many of the characters in the latter are goblin-like, including Uncle Harvey the toad collector and Tubbs and Edward with their local shop—other goblins include Papa Lazarou, who the makers claim, similarly to *The Mighty Boosh*'s more unambiguously problematic Spirit of Jazz, is not an example of blackface but actually a kind of clown or demon—Shearsmith says he based him on the Child Catcher in *Chitty Chitty Bang Bang*, who is quoted by a character he plays in the first episode of *Inside No. 9*. But there is also the taxi driver Barbara in *The League of Gentleman* who is a transphobic depiction of a transwoman, and a caricature of a man attending jobseeker workshops who presumably has a learning disability. *Inside No. 9* picks up the thread of caricature—the character Shearsmith plays in that first episode is a bad queer stereotype—but they seem to move away from their 'taking up' phase towards character acting as time goes on. One of my favourite episodes, which has echoes of *The Shining*, is about the Krampus, a violent beast who comes at Christmas-time to beat children.

Let me pull back the curtain to reveal the wizard and the machinery. As someone who writes experimental fiction, hybrid memoir, and poetry, and who translates contemporary German-language literature, I hope this book shows you can be a writer and *have a laugh, be a laugh.* And have friends. Have your cake and eat it, too. It's like the backlash against method acting—you're not your character, why not just act. I'm acting right now, aren't I, while eating strawberries and sending voice notes of me hissing the word *GOBLINSSSS* to my friend Robin who published a book of my poetry (we do this back and forth to each other). Lermontov looks a bit like the Wizard of Oz and Walt Disney, these men pulling levers, wielding the fog machine. Disney, too, was said to exploit his workers, forcing them to scrap their work, forcing them to overwork, he was anti-union. (Some classic Disney cartoons and episodes of *The Muppets* now have unskippable notices on Disney+ to warn of racism pre-viewing: 'This programme includes negative depictions and/or mistreatment of people or cultures. [...] These stereotypes were wrong then and are wrong now.' This includes yellowface, slurs against Native Americans, racist stereotypes, and white actors mis-voicing Asian and Black characters.)

In Art Review, Jamie Sutcliffe recently wrote a magical article on the unfair labour of cartoonists in so-called 'render farms' for new films like *Teenage Mutant Ninja Turtles: Mutant Mayhem* (four pizza-guzzling goblins who live in a sewer) and *Spider-Man: Across the Spiderverse* (the radioactive spider was the goblin). Sutcliffe quotes Hungarian artist Petra Szemán, a 'self-proclaimed "video gremlin"' whose films and video games are about the sense of self when body and screen merge due to technological entwinement. Szemán is quoted as having said that their 'physical body seems to disintegrate the smoother and fuller the animated one gets; pleasing animation and bodily comfort appear to be inversely proportional to one another', like the cartoon is a cannibal, a Dorian Gray portrait. Bodily breakdown and kids shows don't tend to go together—Bugs, Daffy, Wile E., Tom don't really get hurt. In *Don't Hug Me I'm Scared*, the first episode chucks you out of its kids' show ruse (like when the film *Fresh* goes from romcom to horror film) by revealing a disgusting welt on the body of one of the puppets, then later, the exposed brain of another. Sutcliffe in his article calls cartoons 'serious tricksters' because they hide the reality of labour that went into them: 'Every time Road Runner disappeared into a trompe-l'œil tunnel, Tasmanian Devil evaporated into a scratchy cyclonic gust or Wile E. Coyote rebounded from injury with the immortal elasticity of a bestial Rasputin, you can be sure that something contrastingly static and arduous was happening behind the scenes.'

Phil Fletcher reveals something really interesting about the 'normal men' meme in the Planet Woo article: in their earpieces, Fletcher and Layfield were actually getting shouted at for being unprofessional, with threats that they'll get taken off air. At the end of the article, Alan Roberts, the author of the book *Philosophy of Humour* argues that the meme 'ticks all the boxes' on the four rules for what makes something funny. It's, of course, fundamentally illogical, which ticks box one, but then it also 'occurs in a play setting, raises arousal by going off script, and involves contradictions.'

Roberts continues: 'To my mind the main contradiction comes from the dual interpretation of Hacker as a real character versus as a puppet being voiced by someone cracking up'. This, the article concludes, means that such humour is an 'evolutionary reward for discovering errors in our thinking.' We laugh because we've been fooled. Fooled into thinking a puppet is real and we can relate to it like another person.

Every person we've never actually met but watched online, every person we have met or even knew very well once upon a time but no longer see in real life—either because it feels like too much time has passed, or because the puppet show tricks us into thinking everything's stayed the same—is part of our universe-sized puppet show. On a screen or in a theatre everyone we watch becomes a puppet, a flattened avatar, a case filled with sticks and stuffing; but we feel for them, with them, through them, though still not much for those behind the scenes perhaps. I have friends who are animators, illustrators, theatre directors, who, just like me, are over pushed for creation, creation, creation. We don't talk enough. Instead of liking a meme video, I could instead get in the habit of messaging my friends every Monday morning. Maybe it would be painless.

A few weeks ago @wejustnormalmen posted a thread that began...

'We're just normal men. 100,577 (at time of counting) normal people. Now let's talk about innocence. In Gaza, there are the most heart-wrenching, horrific things happening to innocent children, women and men.'

and ended...

'For those that see this account as an escape, it still will be. This cause is just clearly more important than that. The comfort for such safe havens should not be bought from the purse of perpetual wilful ignorance.'

Another tug on my strings. *Pull your hand out!*

GUTTER

I jolt to a stop on the Queen's Road
bitten nails can't get purchase on
the lip of a depressed manhole cover
insecure, now two halves
a snapped biscuit
it jumps with each passing car
cobbles writhe and shiver
all the paving in the town has broken loose
walking is to play a glockenspiel
slabs clunk with resonance
the yellow brick road once the magic's gone
a rag-and-bone cart makes the cover pop open
I descend into fuggy anti-light
I'm unseen and unseeing
nothing registers, bliss. I wander the pipes
find gigantic avocados and big eggs filled with
rotting dreams. Someone booms
my name at the slick walls, some weak
applause rebounds, I find a ladder *toot suite*.

GOBBLE

ON EATING AND CANNIBALISM

I listen to the same YouTube playlist every day while working.
It's made up of things I've collected over the years. There's some
Cher, Lil Nas X, ABBA, The Strokes, Kate Bush, Manic Street
Preachers, SZA, the Misfits, Elton John, Animal Collective, songs
from the *Labyrinth* soundtrack, novelty *Saturday Night Live* songs,
the Yeah Yeah Yeahs. The playlist grounds me in a strange, muffled
limbo where I don't age yet flit between being a teenager, a kid,
someone in my thirties, someone in my twenties, and where time
passes unremarkably. Every day feels the same, every part of the
day feels the same.

Sometimes wacky adverts, jarring new songs, and
momentous-sounding film trailers come on during the playlist
because I don't want to pay to keep them at bay. They often burst
out of the defined walls of predictability and interrupt my flow
of thought. I was typing away when some quirky incidental music
came on that I didn't recognise. I sighed, it had thrown me off track.
I peeled back the sheet of my document to watch the film trailer
playing in quick, distracting cuts. Two magnetically attractive
people are flirting in a supermarket. A romcom of some kind. What
was it about the trailer that got me? Maybe it's because the ominous
synth chords of "Heads Will Roll" by the Yeah Yeah Yeahs slowly
drones in from a distance. The flirty atmosphere drops away and
is replaced with a sense of dread and illuminati imagery. It must
have been the mesmerising dance between the two leads where
they turn to face me, looking me in the eyes with determined
gazes on their faces. (I rewatched the trailer just now and this is
misremembered; they're looking just off passed the camera.) When
the trailer finished, something happened that I experience when

I find a song I will become obsessed with and listen to to death:
I got a shiver down my spine.

Fresh. I find the trailer and watch it again. Then again. I google
the film. Starring Sebastian Stan (The Winter Soldier from various
Marvel films) and Daisy Edgar-Jones (who has expressed the wish
to become SpongeBob SquarePants and who is best known as
Marianne from *Normal People*). The tagline is 'meat-cute'. It's about
'the horrors of modern dating'. When it finally comes out, I set up
the optimum conditions for viewing. The house is empty, it's the
middle of the day. For the duration of the film, I lived it, I was inside
it. *Na-uh-uh, I'm not going to tell you everything up front, you're going to
have to read on.*

 Post that first viewing, I find that I feel out of sorts,
preoccupied, slightly unwell. I realise I feel like I'm in love. The
film has made me feel like I've started a doomed love affair, it's put
a love spell on me. I pause it in complete shock as the credits finally
come in *after half an hour* (I hadn't realised they'd not opened the
film) accompanied by woozy music to match the feeling of vertigo
you experience when the shocking twist is revealed: Edgar-Jones'
Noa, bewitched by Stan's Steve after meeting at a supermarket and
dating for maybe a week, has been taken away for a weekend break,
stopping first at his surprisingly large and remote house—moments
after sipping her arrival cocktail, she has fallen to the floor, obviously
drugged. You realise you've been duped just like Noa: you're not in
a romcom, my love, you're in a horror film.

 The images from the first soft and gooey part of the film
flicker through my brain like a flip book. I should have seen the

signs—Steve isn't a super cute, awkward and gorgeous reconstructive surgeon, but a cannibal who seduces and kidnaps women so he can sell their body parts for high-end cannibal clients (and have a little snack himself). It's a great metaphor for both finding out your new boyfriend has a terrible hobby you're going to be bored to death with and will have to pretend you like, and that he's a closet misogynist. I realise that I would have easily fallen for Steve. I find this somehow exciting, that I can be tricked so wholly. It's less about the eating people, truly, it's all about the trick. It's about finding out something new about myself. I'm hooked.

In the Guardian's review, where it says that the 'sweet 30 minute romcom' section happens 'audaciously' before the credits, it describes how the film 'quickly switches up to reveal something sour, like biting into a succulent peach that's rotten on the inside', like when David Bowie's Goblin King drugs Jennifer Connelly's Sarah with a bewitched peach in *Labyrinth* in order to make her have weird dreams of dancing with him at a (mildly erotic) masked ball. The moment Steve starts singing in the operating theatre while 'taking (Noa's) ass' to punish her for trying to escape (of course a goblin would steal an arse of all body parts), this is also like *Labyrinth* in that it technically becomes a musical. Then there's the dancing at the end, a miniature ball, the proliferation of mirrors in the film, Steve's hard to reach villa, itself difficult to navigate with its craggy walls, hidden places, intimidating stairs, his oubliette for women, and of course, the end where the whole fantasy that they could be together is destroyed. (Though Sarah gets the baby back; Noa never gets her ass back.)

Even days after watching it, *Fresh* is all I can think about. I'm looking at nothing in particular and mumble to R that the film has had a strange hold over me. I feel glad this film exists, strangely proud of Mimi "Grotto" Cave, its director, who had previously made music videos, the cast and crew, the production company A24, which had already got a delicious reputation for weirder, wilder, hybrid creatures. I watch a making-of video where Cave discusses how they built the set, I watch Stan and Edgar-Jones' joint interviews and photo shoots where the chemistry they have is as palpable outside of the film. *Look at that smile*, R says of Stan/Steve, when I kind of *make us* watch *Fresh* together in a double bill of my choosing, *Fresh* then *Get Out*—they complement one another perfectly, the handsome white man and the beautiful white woman tricksters. "Would you have fallen for Steve?" I ask R, trying to be chill. "I don't know." He replies. "Probably."

Am I just infatuated with Stan's seductive Steve? He represents the goblin of the chauvinist feminist—the guy who's learned all the magic words and moves to cloak his misogyny. He says all the things I've heard before that proved to be treacherous, or even simply words that R said to me or me to him while we were 'dating', 'courting', in those tentative, vulnerable early stages where you mirror the other person, make yourself addictive to them. "I won't text you, but I'll want to"—I'm sure I said this once, too. What's so attractive is he is giving her 100% of his attention. Every bit of it. He gazes at her, but doesn't stare. He listens. You feel that he cannot possibly do or think about anything else except be enthralled by her.

But I also find an energy from him. I wake up the day after watching *Fresh* for the first time more energised than I've been in a long time, eager to do exercise, eager to be confident, to be the main character in my life. Like Patrick Bateman in *American Psycho*, he exercises and cares a lot about his appearance. You have to keep the honeytrap slick, I guess. There is also a furious, repulsive productivity. Steve has a family, spends all day chopping up women, which he's very passion*ate* about, and also dates prospective victims. A goblin can be slovenly and lazy, but they can also be highly motivated. They build castles, they hatch plots, they plan and carry out how they will imprison, nourish, then eat you. After watching *Fresh,* I'm the most productive I've been in about two years. I rewrite a chapter of my PhD, write two articles, and translate about 5000 words within a matter of days. I look at my phone less, and feel like I'm actually living, not living vicariously or hiding away in the mine of my work. I feel so confident, it's infectious, and all from a cannibal! Steve is not on social media, mainly in order to be unfound and unidentifiable of course, but this means he's not busy scrolling his life away! He's too busy, he has things to do. I think to myself 'What Would Steve Do', he wouldn't be on X reading people's opinions. Steve knows social media is killing our minds, a goblin for our attention. Even when very taken by him in the film, you don't quite trust his aloofness to social media, but you know, he gets shit done. He puts away his phone before having his last supper with Noa (admittedly because his wife keeps calling). I sit and read a book without distraction and feel better for it. Thanks Steve.

Fresh could be about the disintegration of a relationship. The bright beginnings and the entrapment that comes ultimately, in the end. In gender roles, in domesticity, in paranoia about exes, the conspiracy of it all. Noa devours the stories of Steve's previous victims, asking if they also got to have dinner dates with him once he ensnared them, while actually devouring one of them together— her ruse to get him to drop his guard through her own switcheroo honeytrap. She frames them in her mouth as ex-girlfriends hidden in the basement (not metaphorically, for real—she's talked through the walls to them), their mementos hidden away for admiration, and those that had a chunk taken out of them before being sent off dismembered, adding to his collection of past conquests. Noa co-eating his victims is like an alternative version of Angela Carter's "The Bloody Chamber" where Bluebeard's new young bride partakes of his murdered former wives hidden in the out-of-bounds room to convince him that she's not like other girls. Steve says that he knew Noa was special from the moment he met her, because she's 'fucked up too'. The lonely goblin sees a co-dependent fairy tale before him. What Steve doesn't get is a woman will eat human flesh and lie to your face that it was delicious, no hesitation, because they've had to self-cannibalise and judge every root of escape no matter the danger. It is in fact not preposterous or unrealistic that Steve can both be the most charming, attentive and thoughtful boyfriend in the world, and also a murderous psychopath. In fact, it's the realistic portrayal of an abusive man, so nuanced in comparison to the public caricature abuser in films, that makes it so painfully real. He would make your friends, your family, your colleagues fall in love with him, as soon as possible after you had, then you would be absolutely trapped. It's clever that the film shows his complicit wife, a presumed former victim who has married him and had his children. We see that any relationship with him, no matter how alluring he seems, would be horrifying—reduced to 'teamwork', a chaste kiss in the bathroom, his wife looking after the home and children while he's out kidnapping and murdering. He starts out a killer catch and ends up entrapping you.

Steve thinks being eaten and doing the eating is a form of love: 'It's about giving, giving yourself over to somebody, becoming one forever'. In the TV show *Hannibal*, Hannibal Lecter and Will Graham's intimacy grows, as does the blurring of their personalities. "If you look at cannibalism throughout history there is something extreme about consuming somebody else," Hannibal opines, "if you love someone fully the most extreme you can go with that is to digest them and make them be part of you." Hannibal is coarser and arguably more immoral and selfish than Steve (in the world of cannibals) because he tricks people into eating his victims by dressing up the flesh of simple folk into fancy gourmet meals; the ultimate superiority complex, when you think someone would be better as feed. We could surmise that Hannibal keeps killing to both hold Will's attention, but also to hold off succumbing and consuming Will/consummating his love for Will—something real serial killer-cannibals are known to have done. (In one of my favourite episodes of the children's show *The Storyteller*, fairy tales that were my Bible stories, a man must cook people he drugs for a griffin to prevent it from losing control and eating whole villages— a small dose of 'manflesh' goulash. Did you know that goulash *[ghoooouuulash]* is the same as hodgepodge? I did not. Did you know that the cannibal creatures in the B-movie horror *Trolls 2* are inexplicably called goblins and not trolls? I did, because

I watched it with friends during our long-running lockdown
movie group.)

Like Hannibal, Steve loves hosting, cooking, eating, wine.
Noa on the other hand eats junk food—we watch her inhale a big
bag of cheese puffs while she works as an illustrator surrounded by
squeezed tubes of paint, and sketches on napkins. Food isn't about
performance and control for her, but just survival, stimulation, and
pleasure. Like Hannibal, Steve is a connoisseur, in other words, a
killjoy. Steve brings Noa meals, invites her to dinner upstairs in his
lair when she behaves. Noa goes from the joys of snacking to Steve
controlling what she eats, and when. Like the tee-heeing Nazi ghoul
Hans Landa in *Inglourious Basterds* when he interrogates Shoshana
over strudel but makes her wait for the cream—"attendez la crème!"
Before Steve makes his move on Noa in the supermarket, Noa sees
an old man peeling the tops off bottles of milk and licking the
cream from them. Steve and Noa would probably have never worked
out anyway; there are gaps in their ages, their wages, their tastes.
Noa eats meat. She says her favourite element of their takeaway
at her apartment while they're dating are the short ribs. "I don't
eat animals," Steve replies with a penetrating look and a sheepish/
piggish/cowing smile, and Noa is made into a gross creature under
this grazing gaze. I've been vegetarian for about three years, but over
the last year I've been craving meat. I stopped eating it for ethical
reasons (I realised that a pig or a cow or a sheep is, *surprise surprise*,
an animal just like my cat Ludo, named after the friend-seeking
monster in *Labyrinth*). Ogden Nash has two tiny poems about eating
animals and their secretions: "The Pig", a pig-blaming ode where
the animal is just the meat it provides which might be seen as big-

heartedness on its behalf, but which the speaker declares stupid—as if the pig has a choice—and a two-liner called "The Cow", line two summarises our bovine friend as just mooing and milk, and no soul between disembodied mouth and udders, as if they were hanging from string. One day while in Borough Market near London Bridge, I couldn't hold it any longer, ordered a container of ribs from a food stall, then sat on the kerb opposite the roastery/café Monmouth and ate them without a single thought entering my head, while office workers and tourists queued for coffee. Noa reacts with a cry of despair, her fingers sticky and stained with barbeque sauce.

Steve's interest in Noa is purely early on in their dating life. Later, after they come to know each other better, Steve visits Noa where he's chained her to the floor in his clinical dungeon—which, with its wall-size sunset print, reminds you of a cheap hotel—and says he's had a hard day, sipping a glass of scotch while she's literally lying on the floor bleeding because of him. At least the Beast listens to Belle's love of books and offers her access to the library. Instead of a drawing pad and pencils, Steve gives Noa women's magazines (where she finds hidden notes in the marginal gutter of an article from a previous victim lost to oblivion). Steve is a goblin, but Noa is more than his match, for very different reasons. If Steve is obviously a goblin for his kidnapping, coveting, cutting and cannibalism, Noa is men's greatest fear: the woman who can fake smile, fake laugh. Oh, and who will murder you for cutting off her buttocks and murdering other women. Noa's manipulation is unforeseeable to him, his cries of "Noa! You lied to me!" after she and two other victims attack him in his own kitchen sound genuinely shocked and hurt. He has made himself vulnerable, as a woman does, and has been hurt/hurt, tenderised/made tender.

It's impressive that Noa goes ahead with her seduction plan after having been locked in a high-end basement for about a week or so with no showering privileges. What about her body, her mouth, *her bits???* Her sloppiness up to this point in her life has perhaps been preparation for being able to style out seven-day greasy hair in order to seduce Sebastian Stan as a total grotbag with just a dab of powder, a brush of mascara and a swipe of lipstick, with not a can of dry shampoo or a wet wipe in sight. This is also hot, though. He finds her so attractive he doesn't care that she's swampy and stewed. Maybe her hair and body had started cleaning themselves, like we're always hearing about. After two weeks we don't have to use shampoo anymore, after a month, we don't need soap. We've ruined our bodies with chemicals, been stripped of our natural oils. It's hot that he accepts her body in a world that offers up women as sanitised avatars.

What initially lures us in with both Noa and Steve? They're that special kind of icky goblin: they woo us with the manic pixie dream girl playbook. Him, with his cotton candy grapes he offers Noa in the supermarket, her with her request to have all the cherries the barman has for her cocktail on their first date. There are tainted callbacks to their dates where they share the bowl of cocktail cherries and the meaty takeaway in the form of the spiked drink with a cherry in it (something Noa calls 'thoughtful', in a slightly mocking voice, as if she already sees through the performative nature of such a thing) and on the trays of food Steve brings Noa in his white basement. The trays are the kind you'd find in a hospital or a school cafeteria. Steve's not your typical lunch lady. (Lunch ladies in cartoons like *The Simpsons* and *Bob's Burger* or in American high school movies are all depicted identically grotesque: 40-cigarette-a-day voice, maybe drunk, serving slop, they join with other women deemed grotesque for being fat or not deemed feminine enough due to their proportions: Heather in *EastEnders*, Brienne of Tarth in *Game of Thrones*, the Trunchbull in *Matilda*, who is evil, but her size and hairiness join up with her evilness.) I have to admit, the food does look irresistible in *Fresh*.

Tray 1
Creamy pasta
A plate of fries
A slice of cake
Short ribs

Tray 2
A cookie
A slice of pizza
Mashed potatoes
Fresh cherries

Oh boy, those homemade reconciliation meals for the unreconcilable sure look good! Oh, to have a writing residency where I could read all day while I'm brought meals, while I take chunks out of myself through my writing.

I love food, and TV shows, and food shows. I spot *The Bear* in the woodland of TV options (a perfect accompaniment). It was probably that slightly goblinoid picture of Jeremy Allen White as Carmen "Carmy" Berzatto (Italian for 'bear' and the pet name everyone in his family has for each other) looking stressed, waiting for someone to release him from his thumbnail oubliette, that drew me to open the trapdoor of the icon. The episode in season 2 called "Fishes" aka "the Christmas episode"—which introduced me to guest star comedian John Mulaney in earnest—is maybe its most stressful. Matriarch Donna (performed with gusto by Jamie Lee Curtis), mother to Carmen and his sister Natalie, is an alcoholic self-medicating for bipolar disorder who gets purposefully drunk and cooks an impossibly elaborate Christmas meal. It's impossible because she drinks, impossible so she can drink, and she berates everyone for not helping while saying she doesn't want anyone to help and that they're doing everything wrong. The episode follows on from one where Natalie finds out she is pregnant (the actress really was pregnant with a *crotch goblin*), and this Christmas dinner memory haunts her because she worries she might become like her mother. In Donna's hands, cooking is control, and controlled love. Food-making as showing love to your children/family but also a kind of swap-out/ersatz/cheaper replacement for care and therapy.

My parents have never been big communicators, or big at expressing affection. Food stood in for both of these. My mum grew up in a poor household, a tiny council house where she lived with her parents and three sisters. They were underfed, undernourished. All the sisters suffered with their teeth from young ages because they ate things like sugar sandwiches. (My friend Barbie sent me a recipe for Goblin Sandwiches from the American pamphlet *How to Run a 1946 Halloween Party:* devilled ham, avocado, Brazil nuts, Worcestershire sauce, inside a sliced doughnut.) Maybe this is the reason my mum went to catering college when she left school. She loved cooking, she loved making cakes. But her mental health became worse and worse, and me and my brother grew up in the 80s and 90s, so we had overdone/underdone oven food for every meal if she was cooking. The feeling of chewed chips sliding at a snail's pace down your throat was like being throttled. And my dad grew up in post-war Malta with rationing extending into the 50s, when he was born. He moved to the UK when he was 19, and having access to lots of affordable food is something he's still not got over, even in his seventies. Being able to buy as much food as you want with the money you have is still a revelation. It means he's always cooked us mountains of spaghetti, heaped mounds of curry with rice, an island of fish pie. It means he makes us a sandwich an hour before lunch or dinner, a huge meal with automatically provided second helpings, and a homemade crumble for afters. Food has always signified love for me. I feed myself treats to let myself know I care. But nowadays the treats come every day, for the smallest milestones. I'm now sick of treats, they're no longer treats, they're nothing. Neither of my parents could really express their emotions. I realise now my parents were famished in ways unrelated to food. Donna's stomach rumbles for appreciation and acceptance, maybe it did before Carmy, Mikey and Nat came along. Maybe since she was a child. But I've always been fed. What more is there to say.

Carmy needs control. He needs it to cope with his past, his present, his family. But Carmy's new sous-chef Sydney soon gets frustrated at the slow progress and steady-shipping Carmy dictates at the restaurant he inherited from his brother Mikey (who, like Donna, battled mental health and addiction problems before he ended his life), and the atmosphere at the restaurant begins to simmer and thicken. Plus the inherited staff act like goblins to Carmy and Sydney, hiding his knife, cranking up the heat on her pot, and this adds to Sydney's rising temperature. She pushes and pushes for The Beef to revolutionise; she puts her new dish of short ribs (Noa would be there in a flash) and risotto accidentally/on purpose in front of a critic—not signed off! But worse than this, she pushes to take online orders, meddles and fiddles, makes faces, but forgets to turn off the pre-order option, causing the orders to stream out of the machine in huge quantities like an overflowing bubble bath (when the bear from darkest Peru does this in *Paddington* I get huge amounts of anxiety, the marmalade sandwich-eating imp), every bubble an order, Carmy shouting, "255 sandwiches, 38 salads, 78 pieces of cake…" (like the drive-thru sketch in *I Think You Should Leave*: "55 BURGERS, 55 FRIES, 55 TACOS, 55 PIES, 55 COKES, 100 TATER TOTS, 100 PIZZAS, 100 TENDERS, 100 MEATBALLS, 100 COFFEES, 55 WINGS, 55 SHAKES, 55 PANCAKES, 55 PASTAS, 55 PEPPERS AND 155 TATERS", or when Bob in *Bob's Burgers* goes to help out at the neighbourhood sandwich shop 77 Sandwiches and helps the owner make all 77 of her different sandwiches for an order on his day off from the burger bar because he has forgotten how to relax).

This online order fiasco scene in *The Bear* featured in the Slash Film column "Scariest Scene Ever" for a reason. Sydney pushed passed the limits of what was sustainable, she what-iffed and what-iffed until she blew the place up. Like Steve, she lets out her frustrations at making an error of judgement by serving Richie (the brash, chaotic, juvenile best friend of Carmy's dead brother Mikey) his ass on a plate, or rather accidentally/on purpose stabbing him in the ass with a knife.

People went crazy for the omelette that Sydney makes Natalie when she's exhausted, stressed and heavily pregnant. It has opposite intentions behind it to Natalie and Carmy's *mom*. There's something very kind about making food for others, especially if there's tension between you, it softens and melts them. Apart from if it's Steve. Or perhaps Alma in *Phantom Thread*, who enrages the particularly goblinine Reynolds Woodcock to the point of him accusing her of being a spy because she cooks his asparagus (*for the hungry boy*) in butter and not oil, and who makes him chatter his teeth together in horror when she drags her spoon across her pearly whites during a honeymoon breakfast. (Steve does this too while eating human meatballs and linguini, eeeee!) Of course, it's when Alma tries poisoning Reynolds with mushrooms that they find their flow—when disarmed for a few days due to toxic fungi, she can find pleasure in dominating him, and he can wallow in a regressed state of helplessness. Woodcock is the Goblin King in his white townhouse, hobgoblin women spinning lace for his haute couture like Rumpelstiltskin (described on Villains Wiki as 'a magical dwarf [or goblin, or imp]-like creature'), who promises Alma a ladder up.

Anyway, how's that omelette coming along? The recipe for the omelette Sydney makes was shared in articles recreating all the food in *The Bear*: The Original Beef of Chicagoland's braised beef sandwich, Mikey's family spaghetti pasta sauce, Marcus' chocolate cake, Sydney's short ribs and risotto.

"I Made the Omelet From "*The Bear*" and Yes, You Should Too"

"*The Bear*'s Omelette Has Chefs Divided"

There was an article titled "A woman, a couple of eggs and a bag of crisps: how an omelette became *The Bear*'s breakout star", going on to say 'It's the egg dish that captured the world's imagination' and that it will be the scene that is remembered for years to come. An omelette upstaged all these actors who just swept award season! Also 'egg dish' sounds disgusting for some reason.

Recipe for Sydney's Omelette:

3 large eggs—on Cursed Commercials Wiki you'll find Egg Man from a 1983 Kinder Surprise advert where Egg Man talks in frantic gibberish, and obviously wishes to cannibalise his Kinder ('choco scrum!', 'me scrobble now!'). You'll find Egg Man's doppelgänger half a century earlier in a 1933 film adaptation of *Alice in Wonderland* (*Labyrinth* is basically *Alice in Wonderland*, isn't it?), which also features an awful eggy man; Gavin Turk's Portrait of an Egg is a crowdsourced exhibition of egg art you can view on his website; Lin in *Bob's Burgers* calls eggs 'delicious bottom diamonds'.

4-5 tablespoons of butter—really gives Alma a run for her money.

A sliver of Boursin cheese—a bonkers advert did the rounds on the internet recently featuring a manic cheese-promoting mascot called Cheddar Goblin vomiting mac 'n' cheese over kids. It turned out it was a fictional advert that appears in a Nicolas Cage film that he watches in his underpants. The ad was a collaboration between puppet maker Shane Morton and Casper Kelly, who made Adult Swim's infamous *Too Many Cooks*. Morton, who made Smarf the Cat for *Too Many Cooks*, had a tripartite inspiration for the Cheddar Goblin: '*Ghoulies* meets Yoda meets Satan'. I think Alan Partridge counts as a cheese goblin—"Smell my cheese you mother!"

A handful of crisps—I wonder if Noa has any cheese puffs left?

Chopped chives—snippets of grass, wild garlic, flecks of mould, snot-ball peas, furry kiwis, oily olives, (especially when stuffed, Craig Raine, a goblin poet, has a line about a stuffed olive looking like it's had a prolapse, my friend and former bandmate Liv [Oh, Liv!] sent me a pimento stuffed olive candle after my mum died), scaly avocado...

Columbo's eggs (which could be a separate essay, 'Columbo's Eggs'! *Just one more thing...* read Rebecca May Johnson's abandoned essay on how Columbo is an omelette-cooking egg in a 'shell-coloured raincoat' who 'cracks' subjects in her book *Small Fires*) are multi-purpose. They add to his disarming grottiness and gruffness, he must leave a trail of shell (not to mention ash) everywhere he goes. He fidgets with them while he thinks and talks to focus his mind. Plus: they're a rich source of protein, which any Lieutenant needs to solve crime. There's an episode with Martin Landau (who won an Oscar for playing Bela Lugosi in *Ed Wood*, and who is unbelievably handsome in his breakout role in Hitchcock's *North by Northwest*; he could play Steve in a remake of *Fresh* in the past) where Landau plays murderous identical twins (!!). The TV chef twin tries to make a fool of Columbo by bringing him on stage during a show and getting him to separate yolks from a dozen eggs. Columbo childishly rocks from side to side as he sloshes the egg from shell half to shell half. Columbo is tongue-tied; usually so unstoppably chatty, he can only say 'um' over and over, smiling in embarrassment as the audience laughs. The twin smugly thinks he has the upper hand, but then Columbo surprises him by revealing backstage that he knows his rich uncle died by electric shock, and it's only a matter of time before he tells everyone that he knows the estranged twins—the TV chef and a bank manager with a gambling problem—worked together to kill their uncle by throwing an electric whisk into his bath, then setting it up to look like he had a heart attack on his electric bike. (I sometimes feel like I'm on an electric bike having a heart attack, when really I'm just answering emails or doing admin or giving talks about being a successful writer when I can barely make ends meet and feel like a failure. I've been teaching many creative writing courses recently, and in the courses I set a timer for writing tasks. 5 minutes, 10 minutes, 15 minutes, 20 minutes. I've started setting a timer for day-to-day tasks too. Yesterday I set a timer for a nap for 6 minutes—the length of time it takes to soft boil an egg.) Ruby Tandoh, the cook and journalist who started her career as a runner-up on *The Great British Bake Off*, wrote an article calling out the fake inclusivity of cooking shows when famous

TV chefs didn't speak out against the Tories in the 2017 general election, including Paul Hollywood (once called an 'albino goblin' by Noel Fielding, who played Old Gregg in *The Mighty Boosh*, whose species classification is widely debated, 'he could be half man half fish' with 'strange seaweed-like hair, webbed fingers and green/scaly skin' who lives in the Black Lake and has a 'frog-like crouch', like a discount Creature from the Black Lagoon). For The Hater column in the online food mag Vittles, Tandoh wrote a takedown of the 'TV Food Man', all those homogenous blokey chefs filling our screens with banter/butter. Another food show contestant (redacted, not for legal reasons, I just don't want his name in my book, into the dungeon with you) appeared on *MasterChef: The Professionals* and played perhaps the most arrogant chef they've ever had come through. When a small independent bakery called Frog opened in Camberwell, he sued them for brand infringement because he claimed people would confuse it with his restaurant by the same name. They changed their name in his honour to Toad. Someone on BlueSky posted about having received a 'Fortnum and Mason's Chocolate Uncommon Toad for Christmas' (tongue-twister)—basically a large, hand-sculpted, impressively mottled chocolate toad—and how they were going to eat it like an ortolan, a bird once considered a delicacy that people would eat whole, bones, beak, and all, with a napkin over their head to hide their modesty/monstrosity. Eley Williams has a short story about it called "Fears and Confessions of an Ortolan Chef" in her collection *Attrib.*, and in *Brooklyn 99*, Charles' fiancée has done this very thing for research purposes as a scholar of food history. (Like the griffin in *The Storyteller* crunching the bones in his goulash like croutons.)

Would I eat a big chocolate toad? (My friend Katie once made me a birthday cake recreating something awful we'd seen in a wildlife documentary, a toad that grows its babies inside its own back: it was a chocolate cake cut into a toady shape, with pistachios as the froglets poking out of it, I wonder if this toad was the inspiration for Gizmo's birthing of the Gremlins?) Or the big chocolate oyster I saw at the posh supermarket? I've eaten chocolate bunnies, chocolate eggs, there's a crème egg in my bag RIGHT NOW in fact, I might eat it for breakfast. The British artist Georg Wilson has an ongoing series of paintings of goblins—plump, scowling and pastel green, where they feast and fight over all sorts of things. A favourite is one where three goblins fight over eggs for breakfast wearing boots and hats, foxes and birds circling them. At her solo exhibition *Gāmboo!* (a Persian word meaning 'greedy, gluttonous, food obsessed'), British-Iranian artist Roya Bahram recently exhibited her trompe-l'œil; appealing food—and some slugs—carved from stone. Treats that could have been made by the Gorgon Medusa for a gaggle of gargoyle mates. The exhibition is 'a celebration of indulgence', inviting the viewer to think 'not just about restriction and guilt, but also about appreciation, pleasure, and even a touch of whimsy.' The food items included a fried egg carved from Cararra and Giallo Siena marble, a slice of glittering brie made of alabaster, and a melted ice lolly fashioned from turquoise soapstone.

Tandoh (can't write Tandoh without t-o-a-d) wrote an immense piece about all the different kinds of ice cream one can find in London, dozens and dozens of them. Eating ice cream as a job! Thinking through the eating of ice cream! In the episode of *The Bear* called "Sundae", Sydney spends the day eating everything, a bit like the Very Hungry Caterpillar. Actually, she begins by googling all the many long-standing food joints that have shut down in Chicago, drank up by the pandemic and rising prices. The new iteration of The Beef, The Bear, is being consumed before it's even tried to exist—it's rotting, it's getting swallowed in the post-pandemic economy. As Agustina Bazterrica argues, capitalism and cannibalism are pretty much the same thing. Carmy and Sydney make plans to travel around Chicago for a palate cleanse (from their test kitchen disasters, and also, you feel, from one another), but Carmy is seduced away by his recently returned school crush Claire (like Steve and Noa, they have a meet-cute in the supermarket). Seeing the manic pixie dream girl trope rear its ugly head again in the form of Claire was a fright. Claire, the doctor who has nothing better to do than call to tease Carmy, be ever-supportive about his stressful restaurant, and seemingly jibe him with no self-awareness at how irritating she is. Hang on: alluring doctor stalking a forlorn pork chop in the supermarket... maybe she's a cannibal! Maybe she's in cahoots with Steve to sell slabs of *short kings!* When Carmy bails, Sydney goes ahead without him and eats all the food all day, more food than one person could eat. In their article on this episode "An Autonomous Woman Is Inherently Destructive", Nicky Beer celebrates the depiction of a woman eating alone—the matter of many think-pieces in recent years—but also a woman eating alone copiously. Beer ponders if the amount of food is purposely a fictitious quantity, or rather an attempt to show a chef or critic's superpower for consumption. The food is abundant, and so is Sydney's imagination. In her mind, her ravioli-pierogi recipe-in-progress splashes around, dances, disappears, has a costume change, reappears, sauces flying. Excessive eating, excessive imagination. Eating as research. Beer also writes in her review that the fact that Sydney eats/researches all day and yet 'there's no "reward" for her thinking' because the final test dish is as terrible as the one she made that morning is a more realistic depiction of creativity than the usual epiphany. Creativity is a slippery creature. You may put the work in, but it can still get away, trick you into thinking you invested enough, before running off cackling.

I just ate a vanilla cream festival bun the size of my face, trying each bit of it, like back when I was a short-lived restaurant reviewer for a website that disappeared overnight for undisclosed legal reasons, but also to think about pleasure, because writing this book feels, to me, like indulging in, no, relishing a cream bun. All for me, but I let you take a bite.

Sydney eats a sundae in a wonderful big scalloped clamshell dish, and part way through she eats the cherry—it's not seductive or flirtatious, she just puts it between her teeth and tugs it off the stalk, it almost looks like she's yanking out a tooth or pulling the pin off a grenade. Noa would have probably asked *for all the cherries*. I imagine all that day's food piled up around Sydney in one go and it makes me think of mukbang videos. These videos are thought to have originated in South Korea, and show men and women eating piles of food. Are they ASMR? They're mic'd-up to the teeth, opening fizzy drinks and pouring them (*glug glug hiss hiss*) into glasses of ice, slurping noodles, crunching fried chicken. Are they erotic? Sucking lobster legs (in *Bob's Burgers*, Bob describes lobsters as 'ugly red sea bugs'), lip-licking, sauce dripping down chins.

As an unpaid sideline I run a small press for Maltese literature with my friend Kat. Kat and I bonded over our Maltese heritage, Sylvanian Families (every time we publish a book, we buy a lucky dip Sylvanian Families baby animal), and a love of treats, especially desserts. Kat and I recently messaged back and forth over Instagram about a tiramisu video:

Slosh in my gob

   Plop in my pie hole

      Slap in my chops

         Whack in my whizzle

            Cram in my kisser

               Yazoo in my yap

                  Jiggle into my jaws

I was writing this book in a café in the upstairs of a shopping centre, where I can hide. They always have tempting cakes, and I'm a sucker for doughnuts especially as I didn't have one (that hadn't been stale, reduced, then frozen and defrosted) until my mid-twenties. I messaged Kat to say:

JC: I'm tempted to have a doughnut

JC: Which I bring up because I think you'll give me permission

KS: Go on you grottlu

Grottlu (grottli, pl.) is Maltese for crab, a kind of hairy crab, but is also used as an insult. When using the word *grottlu*, I think of the Martinware ceramic crab—a 'comical human-faced crab', a grotesque smiling crab with a mouthful of teeth that I loved so much on viewing at a museum, R had it put on a T-shirt as a

Christmas present for me. The author Jean-Paul Sartre hallucinated friendly crabs for years. He would bid them good morning and ask them how they had slept, and would tell them to be quiet and still while he taught at university.

Fresh opens with a shot of a crab in a tank in a restaurant. We first meet Noa on a date with a terrible guy named Chad she met on an app. (While messaging in her apartment with another man on the app whose profile image is a dog, a dick pic suddenly surfaces, looming up out the dark at her—and for a flash, us.) Chad pointedly complains that women hide in baggy clothes and have lost their femininity these days. This mirrors a line later in the film where Steve philosophises to Noa about 'how women just taste better'. Though Steve seems like a chill guy who accepts Noa with her low maintenance and tomboyish style, he brings her a ridiculously anachronistic pink prom dress to wear for their final dinner date. Steve is worse than Chad in this respect; he hid his normative intentions until she was hooked. We hear Chad's droning voice, which Noa's zoning out from, as if underwater, as if he is the crab, the *grottlu*. In a translated novel Kat and I published, the original novel used '*grottlu*' to describe a man and we roped in R to come up with some more derogative options for the translator to consider: Prick? Scum, sleaze, sleazeball, slimeball, slob, weirdo? Dirtbag, pervert, pig? In the fantasy film *Legend*, the pig man says of love interest Lili: 'I could eat her brains like jam', like her head is a doughnut. (Chaos goblin Eric André was recently spotted behind the counter of Manchester doughnut shop Siop.) There are many piggish men and beings, gobliny in their piggishness. There's the pretty harmless, like Shaggy and Scooby in *Scooby-Doo*, Bender the

Robot in *Futurama*, lasagne fiend Garfield, picnic-snatchers Yogi and Boo-Boo. In *King of the Hill*, Hank despairs because his son Bobby gets gout from eating organ meats 'the boy's not a ghoul'! There's a *Simpsons* "Treehouse of Horror" episode where Homer self-cannibalises and it's truly horrifying, sickening, where Homer's head is a ring doughnut. There's another where Homer becomes a blob—"You won't eat my stuffed peppers," Marge complains, "but you'll eat our son!" Homer eats teenagers, a bunch of Germans, when he eats people they dissolve in a fizzing, bubbling pop inside him. He eats the homeless to help society somehow, homeless people are goblinified. In art, too, there are some fantastic pigs, Paula Rego's *Prince Pig* for instance, a pig man who is denied by two sister fiancées, but when accepted by the third sister turns out to be a handsome man, a version of the *Hans My Hedgehog* story told in an episode of Jim Henson's dark series *The Storyteller*. And then there are the tremendous gobblers. There's *The Ricotta Eaters* by Vincenzo Campi where a bunch of grotesques—inspired by Commedia dell'arte figures—spoon runny cheese into their toothy mouths, and my friend Elliot sent me *Goblin with Christmas Porridge* by Edvard Munch where, for some reason, a goblin is celebrating Christmas by shovelling slop into his gob. They could have gained a great following on YouTube. Mukbang videos remind me how the quality of food looks so much better abroad. Touring in bands in Europe was depressing in that we found out that in France, Germany, Spain, they believe that everyone deserves at least high-quality staples for a few euros. Here we have our salty Styrofoam white bread, our plastic chicken. All the food here feels fake. I make salt dough ornaments of food while watching films when

I can't bear to write or translate anymore—cakes, pizza, doughnuts, fried chicken. Though I'm vegetarian (bar those ribs, bar some accidental fried chicken, bar a recent steak), I've watched a lot of strangers eating chicken wings on mukbang videos. After watching *Fresh,* I searched for 'Sebastian Stan interview' on YouTube, and up popped *Hot Ones*, an interview series with celebrities where they eat progressively spicier chicken wings. In Stan's episode he's promoting *Pam and Tommy* where he plays Mötley Crüe drummer Tommy Lee (he has a monologue with a prosthetic puppet penis) and *Fresh* and is wearing some kind of hip version of those flame shirts. He says little of note. As often happens when I watch actor interviews, I find out he doesn't have the style of his characters or red-carpet appearances... Steve died for me a little that day. It did get me onto *Hot Ones* though. I've now gone on to watch many well-known people eat chicken wings while being interviewed. Though the ruse sounds silly, they're some of the best interviews you'll see. Not only is Sean Evans a fantastically prepared, modest and calmly neutral interviewer—unlike most hosts who vie narcissistically for attention with their guest—the interviewee slowly loses control of their faculties (and even body). *Hot Ones* then led me onto *Chicken Shop Dates*, Amelia Dimoldenberg's YouTube show with nugget-sized interviews with musicians and actors where she interview-dates them in London's chicken shops. Dimoldenberg is a chimera, an illusion, a mirage, a mermaid. ("Fuck Ariel!" Noa and her best friend shout at boxing class, *punch, punch,* "Fuck the Beast! I am the Beast!") Dimoldenberg's show opens with stop-motion animation of felt chicken nuggets and, though glamourous, she honestly loves *Wallace and Gromit*—the cheese-consuming sprite and his fairy dog-lifesaver.

Like Sean Evans, Dimoldenberg is completely disarming and open. But unlike Sean, she flips a switch where suddenly her dates feel like they need to impress *her*. She bewitches them, makes them squirm. Maybe the worst episode of each chicken-based show is when Amelia and Sean interview each other on their respective shows. Both of them gave nothing away, and they both seemed uncomfortable—too much was at stake/steak! Doppelgängers should never meet, it was uncanny. I can see Noa and Sydney, or Daisy Edgar-Jones and Ayo Edebiri, having some chicken nuggets and chips with Amelia:

Amelia: So, what do you think of Jeremy Allen White's Calvin Klein commercial / Do you think you and Carmy will get together in the end?
Ayo / Sydney: That's my colleague! This is a work function!

Daisy / Noa: Do you want anything to eat?
Amelia: I've got my chicken nuggets and Mirinda Orange / "Just you," as Steve would say.

Ayo Edebiri called out how inappropriate it is to ask her about her colleague in his underwear at an award's ceremony press junket. Just because it's a party, it doesn't mean she's not working. On the subject of Jeremy Allen White, however, I am working, but in no way am I professional, so I can say that I found the CK ad quite mesmerising for complex reasons. For many people, White appearing in the world of culinary magic feels like a reincarnation of not simply Gene Wilder (birthname Jerome Silberman, who chose his new moniker so he could be... *wilder*), but specifically Wilder as

Willy Wonka, the greatest confectioner in film (though I want to give a shout out to Juliette Binoche's mischievous sprite Vianne's concoctions in *Chocolat*, and Dick Van Dyke's clumsy and chaotic Caractacus Potts' toot sweets in *Chitty Chitty Bang Bang*, one of the best sweet films to rival *Willy Wonka*, which came out three years later in 1971—don't forget the breakfast-making contraption, cooking sausages and eggs by directing flames under a cold plate of raw egg and meat!). But in *The Bear* it's not White's Carmy who's creating magical chocolatey things like his Wonka-doppelgänger (say that five times fast), he's too savoury, in fact, he's too salty. It's Marcus the pastry chef, played by Lionel Boyce, who's transfixed by perfecting his chocolate cake, the kind you would find in *Matilda* but sliced up nicely for the whole school and *NOT* force-fed to a child. It's Marcus proving buns in his plastic-cloaked grotto in a dark corner of the restaurant where he has started sleeping to save time. Marcus smiles at doughnuts through a bakery window, draws them, tastes them, squishes them in his hands. He is gripped by patisserie and brings smiles to people's faces. Marcus' mum is dying, and he cares for her. Marcus' mum is dying, but he has to leave for Copenhagen, the birth-nation and death-city of Hans Christian Andersen, to learn sweet magic. Tina, the softened sweary prankster goblin, is sent off too, to catering school. She is like Cinderella in a white gown at the ball, from scrubbing her section, to learning good knife skills. You shall go to the pass!

In an edited-out shot, you'd see my mum behind Tina in the background at catering college learning (to be) something new. You might see my dad in a cut scene in *Fresh* as a guy in the warehouse where the meat products are processed. My dad's first job when he first moved here was working in a frozen food warehouse. As a teenager I worked at Somerfields supermarket where I had to use the meat slicer, slicing jellied tongue, slicing Billy Bear's pink face. I had to climb into the chicken rotisserie oven to clean it, like the witch in *Hansel and Gretel*, afraid someone might shut me in and roast me. My mum was dying her whole life, since her overly sweet childhood. My dad left too much unsaid with his dad, and it's gnawing away at him. I realise that they've spent their lives being slowly chewed up by their own feelings. I've been finding my parents all-consuming lately, or maybe ever since those meat slicing, chicken roasting days. They eat you up, your mum and dad.

I'm still sucking on that music playlist like an everlasting gobstopper. It tricks my brain into thinking it's full.

GORGE

Out the sewer like a jack-in-the-box
I've ended up downriver in Rye, I spy
a shop, the window full of cream buns
boils, breasts, buy one then
saunter to the bathroom
lock the door, crack open the stiff box in the airless cell
astride the toilet seat I watch myself eat in the mirror
foamy imprints of cream on my cheeks
until the end, splash this soap from my face
on the street I smell meat, the ribs sing to me *juicy sweet*
the flesh unhugs the bone
my reflection in the foil lid is chopped ham
chuck away the evidence, topple after it into the bin.

GAG

ON MISCHIEF

R thinks I've finally gone too far with this goblin stuff and draws the line at clowns being goblins. "Clowns are clowns." Sure, of course clowns are clowns. But clowns are like jesters, jesters are twisty and bendy and mischievous, clowns are creepy, jesters are sneaky, ergo, clowns are goblins. But wait! I have hard evidence, or at least soft back-up. There was an article that set out why clowns are so terrifying. The article was in the style of a back and forth between someone with coulrophobia (the fear of clowns) and someone who, as we read on, we discover to be a clown when they give a *honk*. The article on clowns cites new research from the University of South Wales, where they asked participants in their study to fill out 'The Fear of Clowns Questionnaire', which partly tried to establish the scale of their discomfort with clowns, and it helped them find the eight causes of *ye olde fear o' clowns*, including 'the way that clowns' make-up makes them look not quite human [did you know that clowns have to paint their make-up on an egg to send to the Clowns International Egg Registry?], the implicit threat in their exaggerated facial features and their inherent unpredictability.' What does that remind you of?

When R said that a clown is not a goblin, this statement was followed by him saying, "*unless...* it would have to be something pretending to be a clown," in an offhand way. He cites the film *It*, where It is actually a giant spider dressed as a clown. Villanelle, the assassin in *Killing Eve*, also commits a murder (double murder) while dressed as a clown at a kid's party. One of the other primary causes of clown phobia is due to negative media depictions. Goblins have had a bad rep, too.

Something pretending to be something else—how mischievous, how devious. There are filters online where you can have a clown's make-up overlaying your face, usually shared with a caption saying you had been tricked, sometimes by a partner or an employer, making you into a fool. (There's also a filter that makes it look like you're snogging Shrek.)

In *Animal Joy*, a goblin's delight, Nuar Alsadir combines her expertise in both psychoanalysis and clowning. Clowning and laughter, she argues, help us access the unconscious and the unsocialised self. She quotes Nietzsche—clowning can help you 'become the one you are'—but also her young daughters, whose growing use of humour to challenge power dynamics helps her better understand how messing around is important for our development, and understanding of our self, as well as a tool to negotiate the world and our place in it. In one section of the book, she tells an anecdote about having a blocked ear and her daughter witnessing a spider crawling out of her head. When her daughter makes a joke about it later that day, she sees this laughter as a mechanism to limit the fear of the incident and to cut her mother down to size.

When I think of 'animal joy' I think of something else that honks other than a clown. In *Untitled Goose Game*, a computer game where you are a naughty goose causing mischief, your tasks include stealing washing from a line and throwing it in a pond, stealing a boy's glasses, and shoplifting in a quaint English village, all with a feathery nonchalance and jarring honk. This goose could be a relation of Pingu, "he is a nuisance," my friend Helen says, and also brings up the body horror of *Pingu*—his brother flips a table into his face and *blood drips in big plops from his beak! Pingu* feels like a proto-*Simpsons*, the violence and mishaps and mischief, the sibling love and bullying. *Honk-honk!* In his essay "Everyone needs to grow up" in Dazed, James Greig charts and laments the self-infantilisation of adults—what writer Josh Cohen refers to as 'a retreat into the dubious comforts of a pseudo-childhood' in the piece—that Greig believes makes them disempowered, apolitical, unethical, and even more liable to fall for the trick of fascism: 'Make no mistake: the capitalist elites want you to think of yourself as a silly little goose.' He begrudgingly recognises that the reason why so many people in their twenties, thirties, etc. are craving toys, YA fiction and Marvel films, could be due to not having had proper childhoods or because it's harder for our generation to achieve the typical, normative milestones. Greig brings in Cohen again referencing Freud on the idea that this regression is 'a kind of identification with one's own powerlessness, and so gives it a veneer of active choice':

> Freud pointed out that when small children play games, they are often re-enacting a traumatic situation with the aim of exerting control over it. I can't bear it when mummy leaves, so if I throw this puppet on a string and pull it back, I'll be in control of when she leaves and when she returns.

Being a grown up for a second, I do think Greig makes good points, I think he would hate this book, my hand puppet, but I'm going to *honk* at the idea that we always have a choice to be responsible, to be happy, that our motivations are always obvious to ourselves, that the tools and support are always at hand. And why can't things be two things? Why is the activity of seeking out a second chance at childhood or simply wanting to prolong the benefits of remaining childlike mutually exclusive from doing good in the world, being responsible, being ethical, making change— thinking now of close friends who do jobs that are stressful and vital who enjoy 'childish things', maybe practising both keeps a sense of balance, perspective, the chance to experience a genuine state of rest and connection to self? Anyway, back to me raking over my youth like an archaeologist working at night by the light of a TV set...

One of the first and most memorable pieces of art I ever saw was a Bruce Nauman film installation called *No, No, New Museum* from his Clown Torture series, a 1987 piece comprising two televisions on top of one another with a green and red jester trapped in each one (the top TV had the jester the right way up, the bottom upside down) and they were both jumping up and down and shouting *NO, NO, NO, NO, NO*. Watching it now it reminds me of Don Logan in *Sexy Beast: NO, NO, NO, NO, NO, NO, NO*, and generally of all those modern jesters, Mr Blobby at King Noel's House Party, the dancing Mask compelled to P-A-R-T-Y in his zoot suit, Deadpool, whose biggest weapon is his humour. I found Nauman's film on YouTube and people had commented underneath the video that they too had seen it as a teenager at Tate Modern and that it had haunted them. The description under the video highlights that though nothing bad happens, just a man in bad make-up jumping up and down and pettishly shouting *NO*, there's something innately disconcerting about it. Three of my favourite literary court jesters are Jeremy Noel-Tod, Imogen West-Knights and the duo The White Pube, they entertain the court in the kingdom of social media.

Jeremy Noel-Tod—an associate professor of creative writing and a *twin*—constantly puns and quips, riffing on everything from the most contemporary poetry to the accidental poems of newspaper headlines, to responding to news items and memes with corresponding bits of poetry, to discussing the latest literary scandals, sub-tweeting poets, and using turns of phrase and idioms so hyper-new some teenagers might not have fully grasped them yet. A few recent cuts:

Picture of Ryan Gosling's Ken inserted between Einstein and Oppenheimer
Your A-levels

*Picture of W. G. Sebald's *The Rings of Saturn**
His job is beach

Picture of two men holding up slabs of Kendal Mint Cake with a happy faced mascot between them
She's everything. He's just Kendal Town FC's massive humanoid Kendal Mint Cake mascot

When I first came across his account, I found his posts *silly,* inclusive, and welcoming as a beginner writer for being indiscriminately joyful about language and culture, unlike the majority of academics who are interested in nothing more than defining what culture is, what's worthy, and gatekeeping what 'real poetry' is and can be. At the moment Noel-Tod is locked into writing "Roses are red…" limericks reverse engineered from a final line found in the wild. His one for Valentine's Day this year was based on a poster I sent him advertising a cook book event in Rye:

Roses are red
Horses do gallops
Between you and me
'Tim Anderson Talks Scallops'

One of his claims to fame is pointing out in a review of Simon Armitage that the poet often ends his poems with two phrases spliced by a comma, and Armitage admitted on Desert Island Discs that this gentle trolling made him take notice of what Noel-Tod had called a 'patented sign-off' that was like 'a rock guitarist nodding to the band' and change it.

One day Noel-Tod was joined at court by an account called Bougie London Literary Woman. The short-lived account mocked a certain kind of middle and upper middle-class literary or publishing person and those who cling to the cultural capital of books and publishing, and it was *fucking wicked*. In an article where she explains how the account came about following a crescendo of fascination, backlash and conspiracy, West-Knights says that 'my friend and I used to spend our evenings staying up too late drinking tea, and inventing characters for fun. It's difficult to explain why we do this, but we do. I guess that's the nature of close friendship: you do odd things together.'

Oh how I *miss it*. There were the RSVPs for a plant funeral directed to the London Library to avoid 'feline nibbling', turning down Radio 4 to 'appreciate the murmur' of 'simmering quinces':

Thanking certain dear hearts for a truly scrumptious trove of presents this year. Folio Society treasures, a yearned-for Tove Jansson print, and, at long last, a loom.

My twenty-eighth birthday looms… plotting a trip to the seaside with the coven to shuck oysters and clutch each other's hands.

Wild about my new culottes, which will be just the thing for flaneusing around Broadway Market in search of intrigue and bluebells Sunday week.

This lambasting of literary cottagecore touched a silken, Toast-jacketed nerve, and many of the most unctuously upper-middles in publishing decried it as offensive, misogynistic, obviously written by a man. West-Knights says in her article that the duo did it as middle-class literary people themselves for a laugh, to poke fun at parts of themselves, and because they had identified a persona that had been formed and performed on social media. (Naomi Klein writes that our online profiles are our 'digital doppelgangers [sic], our 'Digital Golems'.) West-Knights acknowledges that it would probably have been very different if it had been a man writing these posts, and it seems to have influenced why she revealed them to be the Bougie London Literary Women.

The White Pube—Gabrielle de la Puente and Zarina Muhammad—cut deep into self-aggrandising criticism with a big C that is often just PR and lip service with their no-nonsense, all-fun art, video game and literature reviews that are rigorous, chatty, tender, and inflected with the language of the internet, the space that gave them and others a voice and platform in criticism; even their name is a send-up of the antiquated, aging, white, serious art world. Their manifesto *ideas for a new art world* was pasted up on billboards, street awnings, and in art galleries, like goblins giving those lurking in comfort a bump and a fright in broad daylight:

001: if I were the Tate, I would simply remove my racist paintings x

004: people across the creative industries need to declare if they have rich parents who helped them get where they are today.

A computer can't (shouldn't) come up with a meme or a witty retort, these human epiphanies, these hybrid moments. (Notoriously unfunny clown Elon Musk thinks his open AI—built from scraping Twitter/X—called *Grok* will be funnier than comedians.) AI might feel compelled to attempt to build composite tweets by analysing the tweet history of a hundred posh publishers, but they would need to be post-edited by a goblin editor to make them have a consistent voice. Hang on, no, wait, let me make clear that AI does not *feel compulsions* and does not undertake *a process of trial and error* until *satisfied* ('gruntled' is an actual word for satisfied), *riff with a friend over tea* (making the attempt also a memory and an experience) as *a form of self-reflection* and in order to *make themselves and others laugh*; it can only be *instructed to complete a task* without any context or desire.

I'm the first to acknowledge that English is a total goblin, and I, like others, rely on help from autocorrect and spellcheck and the internet. I mean, have you seen the word *eighth* lately? I write a column for the Brixton Review of Books about literary translation and translated literature. Sometimes I use my columns to publish excerpts from my forthcoming translations, and my editor, Michael Caines, queried the word 'plane' in describing a fiery scape in a character's dream, asking if it shouldn't be 'plain'? I replied: "Argh, shows what I know about words! Your call is the best call," but sent him what I had found:

This spiritual, *transcendental plane* is the plane of eternal life.

In addition to the devils, this *plane* was home to bonespears, gathra, haraknin, hell hounds, imps, night hags, nightmares, and maelephants.

He responded: "Love the devils, night hags et al—what a dirty trick the English language is playing here. 'Plane' for another level or dimension in some sense. 'Plain' for a cowboy. (Not-so-plain Calamity Jane.) I hope this is the right way round!"

AI is also demonstrably biased and autocorrect can be despicable: turning *fucks* into *ducks* like a magician shoving a rabbit back into his hat. Technology companies are shredding people's confidence in their own writing and individual sense of self under the guise of empowering them. In the documentary *10 Years with Hayao Miyazaki*, the Studio Ghibli head is shown to be disgusted by animators using AI to create a jittery humanoid crawling and sliding along the floor presumably for a horror computer game, finding it dehumanising and ableist—he believes that 'we humans are losing faith in ourselves'. AI is a goblin that wants to convince you that you can't write, *here, let me do that essay on that book you loved and have unexpressed feelings about for you;* that you can't write properly, *here, let me correct those not-even-errors and quirks of your speech in this email to your boss for you;* and that you can't learn a language, *here, let me make you think foreign languages are just a terrible inconvenience and not linked to a culture or people with this non-translation that's just built with similar real and non-real translations,* or choose to be haunted by the green owl of Duolingo and its demands. In the future-or-now, AI is at risk of turning reviewing and other cultural writing into the stuff of algorithms and taking the idea of objective quality to its ultimate endpoint. *This song has similar soundwaves to this popular song. This painting looks like this derided painting. This poem scored highly from our Preferred Words List but poorly on the Sonnetometer for form. This film scored 50% when compared against our ten-point Greatest Films of All Time criteria.* All based on surface level comparables, not inklings and surmises. Rating aggregators like Rotten Tomatoes (remember when *Attack of the Killer Tomatoes* was still bouncing around, about scientist Dr. Putrid T. Gangreen and Tara Boumdeay who was a hybrid tomato-human disguised as a girl?) and Goodreads (where someone wrote my pamphlet *Goblins* was 'Pretentious British art pixie gibberish') are not perfect, or even very nice, and can get played and become gamified, but there are at least gooey humans behind them.

I only want writing made by a human, not necessarily for the writing, but because of what's behind it; where it came from, what it took someone to start it (incredible), rework it (unbelievable) and complete it (miraculous). The human will to write and share one's idiosyncratic ways of thinking, feeling, and then communicating it to others *takes guts*. An AI can't relate its criticism or any writing back to its childhood, its influences, its whims. It wants to standardise, it wants to prioritise information, it can only live in the very adult present. It can't share those embodied, human knowledges that a certain key change makes a shiver run down your spine, or a lyric reminds you of something your friend said once. While watching the making-of documentary about the recent series created as a prequel to Jim Henson's 80s film *The Dark Crystal*, it was comforting to see backdrop painters, puppet fabricators, prop makers, puppeteers, story writers together in a room with note cards, talking about growing up with Jim Henson's creations and/or with parents who were puppeteers (like Toby, the baby from *Labyrinth*, who is now a puppeteer and who worked with his parents on the series).

How to fight AI? Let weirdos write their weird books about how everything's a goblin, full of emotions, nostalgia, personal associations, feelings, memories, that goes off on one, that goes round the houses, that replicates a juicy brain. When I read Todd McEwen's *Cary Grant's Suit: Nine Movies That Made Me The Wreck I Am Today* and *This Young Monster* by Charlie Fox (who once dressed as a black metal troll doll during a panel discussion about Diane Arbus) they could have been writing about anything—it's the way I can feel a person behind the writing that compels me. Aim to write things an AI could never. Culture happens in the home, paraphrasing Roland Barthes, and if culture gets disconnected from feeling and life then it's not culture at all, it's just marketing.

The boom in personal essays might have come from journalists and other writers having to drain their own wells, emptying our pockets of shiny things and lint and saying: *I can bleed for you if you give me the chance!* The way I see it, I land on both sides. I want criticism to be weird and hyperpersonal because the only thing I can really be sure of or an expert in, the focus of all my research and its aims, is myself/my self. But if we feel like we have to give away everything that's personal, turn it into the USP of writing on other things, do we dehumanise ourselves somehow? I forget sometimes that most people do not incorporate themselves into their work, talk about or draw on their life and their experiences every day. They must see me, I realise, as some kind of goblin gawping into a mirror or spitting out in the street. But I stress myself to accentuate my humanity. The thing is, it's both me and not me. This *thing* in your hands is not me. You might think you know me, but you don't, I'm completely unlike any of this. My writing voice, my writing self, is my doppelgänger, one I can conjure, like a model I can build. (Laurie Anderson had Lou Reed made into a chatbot, she thinks it's worth it for the few moments it sounds like him.) As with my writing, which I always naturally make hybrid, my life's pursuit is to remain hybrid myself. I want to subvert expectations, subvert conventions, subvert the genres I've been handed at birth.

I love all things that trick and thrill for not keeping within limitations. Not everyone likes subversion, though, and it also doesn't always work. Todd McEwen writes about reenacting *The Wizard of Oz* with friends as a child but there was a 'no genre-bending' rule, their playing had to be straight up; he also apologises in advance for possibly boring people by talking about *The Wizard of Oz* after it's been written about and 'grave-robbed' by practically billions of 'Judy Garland ghouls'. Her daughter Liza Minelli is a wonderful goblin among the family of goblins in *Arrested Development*, and I just watched a video of her being handed a huge slice of chocolate cake and saying, "That's a helluva piece." I can see the connection between McEwen and friends' reenactments and his cultural criticism. He re-enacts his experiences with cultural artefacts as an adult in essays, but as a child, our ways of understanding a story are through its reenactment, through playing. Someone once said that criticism was like 'making two Barbies kiss'. A meme is a form of cultural essay—finding an artefact and linking it back to something personal or social or political. Criticism can be the juxtaposition of pictures and quotes from *Fleabag* and *Bojack Horseman* (as someone has done) and I think that's swell. *The Little Prince*, it's been argued, is actually philosophy (stuff can be two things!) Or stuff can be three things! Four things! But it can just as much feel like a novelty and a cop out. In an article titled "*Sugar* and the Challenging Art of Genre Hybrids", Colin Farrell's foray as a blue alien detective is dissected and probed, and reports disappointing findings.

How are *The Bear* and *Succession* comedies, articles decried. How is *Don't Hug Me I'm Scared* a comedy? How is *Beef* a comedy? Is *Fresh* a comedy? We're scared when something dark makes us laugh. For Nuar Alsadir, the definition of laughter is truth. *Beef* could be a romcom, the same way that *Fresh* is a romcom, but it's one that ramps up on inequality, repressed trauma and abnormal relations to your loved ones. *Beef* sneaks one of the best moments of experimentalism in a mainstream-but-not show ever. In the final episode, both central characters, Amy and Danny played by Ali Wong and Steven Yeun, who have been antagonists for the duration, speak in unison, in one voice, underpinning that both their rage comes from the same places: the pressure and alienation of being a second generation Asian-American and feeling underappreciated in your family. But actually, maybe *Sesame Street* is the best instance of sneaky experimentalism in film? Jim Henson wanted to be an experimental filmmaker, he was even nominated for an Oscar (The Grouch?) for his short film *Time Piece*, which is a surreal and absurd montage of seemingly unrelated scenes starring a young and handsome Henson with a ticking clock throughout, which reminds me of the chiming clock in *Labyrinth*; Henson made all the experimental animations in *Sesame Street*, which came from his earlier work in film and creating handmade stop-motion visualisations for music when he thought he was going to go into designing the interiors of nightclubs. Henson's life would have ended up very different. Mere seconds after the blood curdling, heart-stopping scream from Eve as she sees Villanelle, her nemesis turned lover, get shot in *Killing Eve*, THE END signposts the show's final destination. What an ending! Shock non-ending! *I May Destroy You*'s formal subversion also comes at the end. We're given three alternative endings but instead of satisfying our goggling gaze for closure, we have to live with the fact that none of them really happened, that none would be satisfying, and that, as with being a victim of sexual violence, there is often no closure.

Then there are creative works that are a joke because they don't convince anyone. When *Maestro finally* finished I said in the deadened tone that felt fitting for the deadened feeling I'd held for the entire length of the film that "Bradley Cooper really thinks he made a film". You could see the thinking, the draft, the shorthand and headline behind every scene in *Maestro*—dancing, *tick*, angry monologues, *tick*, the scene where he conducts (and he told everyone about, watch this bit!), *tick*. You could see the pencil marks and the stitches. The trailer was a more successful, cohesive film. The trailer to another Oscar-nominated film, *Past Lives*, is a perfect two-minute twenty-four-second film. The actual film *Past Lives* was not a film. You can't trick me with minimal dialogue and long silences. (On the extensive film blog Screen Goblin, I read about how Arnold Schwarzenegger is 'at peak gormless' in *Conan the Barbarian*, a film with 'only occasional dialogue, perhaps to make it easier to export, but this comes at the expense of understanding what's happening in the meandering story, which is peppered with revelations from magic scrolls we're told nothing about'.) Watching films on TV, the shiny goblin in my grotto, rather than in the cinema, must be the issue? Nope, I watched *The Zone of Interest* in my living room with regular speakers and felt like I was inside the film. *Ripley*, the latest adaptation of Patricia Highsmith's novel *The Talented Mr. Ripley*, also felt like a trick when I watched it—black and white and deadpan, wooden acting and silence and overwhelmingly distracting cinematography. Admittedly, I might have written it off too soon, but it took me a fortnight of thinking about it for me to see something deeper behind it. Firstly, Andrew Scott's Tom Ripley is almost Dracula-like in looks and constantly exposed demeanour— thinking of him as a vampire in a black and white Italy suddenly made it a far more appealing horror film. I also redressed my feelings about Scott being the completely wrong choice for the role. Where Matt Damon is young, handsome and magnetic in *The Talented Mr. Ripley* (directed by Anthony Minghella, who directed *The Storyteller*, and edited by Walter Murch, who directed *Return to Oz*), Scott is too old for the character, too uncharismatic to be a con artist. But what if we look at these two adaptations through the lens of Humbert

Humbert in Nabokov's *Lolita*? What if Matt Damon is Tom Ripley as he fantasises himself to be—irresistible and in control— as Humbert depicts himself in writing about his "seduction" of Delores, and Andrew Scott is Ripley as he actually is—clearly creepy (Marge in *Ripley* clocks him right away), cack-handed (he nearly drowns while trying to kill Dickie Greenleaf), lucky because he is assisted by police incompetence (they fail to seek out a photo of Dickie Greenleaf and fall for the now infamously terrible disguise Andrew Scott wears in *Ripley*) rather than any expert abilities, just as we know that Humbert Humbert is not a heroic romantic but actually a tragic, delusional and erratic paedophile? I still prefer *The Talented Mr. Ripley*, it's a romp, whereas *Ripley* feels like a perfume advert.

One comment under a trailer for *Saltburn* said that it would have been better off as an exhibition of nice photography, and I understood what that meant completely, even without watching the film. (I'm never going to watch *Saltburn*, but I'm going to talk about it here anyway.) The commenter called Ivelina Ivanova said: 'Great cinematography but the plot is duller that [sic] anything I've seen. This movie should have been an exhibition of photographs with exquisite shots/scenes. The 'shocking' scenes are there just to pinch you to have the illusionary feeling there is something to see, expect or be excited about. Well, a waste of time, overall.' All surface, no depth, no attention to story, script, or arc. Maybe this will be what all movies are like in the future, just imagery, by committee, by algorithm. The problem might also be that the writer director of *Saltburn*, Emerald (green) Fennell (green) is from a very privileged upbringing. She has perhaps been fast-tracked through her creative journey before it could mature. The same with Bradley Cooper (green). Emerald worked on the first series of *Killing Eve* with fellow upper-middle-classer Phoebe Waller-Bridge (writer-star of hot mess *Fleabag*), and this might be why the character of Carolyn, the posh spy daughter of a posh spy—is so good, so emotionally deadened. She seems linked to Rosamund Pike's *Saltburn*ing mother.

There's something a bit Cindy Sherman about Rosamund Pike—she is *Gone Girl* after all. (In *Black Meme*, Legacy Russell reminds everyone—as Margo Jefferson and others have done before—that Sherman appears in a series of her photos in blackface; something not brought up in the documentary R and I watched recently, I felt duped when I learned this.) It cracked me up when Amelia Dimoldenberg went full Sherman and became unrecognisable as gremlin-alien Mr. Bean one Halloween. A poster called @serephfem wrote 'i do not like mr. bean. sinister little man disgusting mischief and evil doing as comedy. He has sickened me since i was a child.' My brother loved Mr. Bean when we were kids— he would buy *Mr. Bean* magazine and Mum knitted him Mr. Bean's faithful bear Teddy. Mr. Bean's naïvety and disastrous curiosity reminds me of Frank in *Some Mothers Do 'Ave 'Em*, characterised as a 'maladroit'; someone 'inefficient or inept; clumsy'. Frank Spencer's inheritors are Stath from *Stath Lets Flats*, frustrated and keen and loving but who is completely unable to work, and Mandy from *Mandy*, who can't retain a job. All three are useless in a capitalist society, we can refigure them as labour saboteurs, and therefore worth cherishing.

I love it when Mr. Bean/Rowan Atkinson gets that screwed up face, bottom lip stuck out, over the most minor things, he looks like Little My, who lives among the Moomins in the books by Tove Jansson. She is small, determined, mischievous and fiercely independent and partly based on the author herself. She is described on the Moomins website as having a 'sharp tongue, quick temper and mischievous nature', who is sometimes shown with a green outline and in a green dress in illustrations. R got me a toy Little My because he says I look like her sometimes, when I get *that look*. My friend Katie drew a picture of me once where I have those same meeting eyebrows. I got My-ified. I like it when friends make fun of me—my moody nature, my inability to evolve with technology, that I misunderstand very simple concepts, "For someone so intelligent you can say some stupid things sometimes," one of my oldest friends told me recently, and I loved it. You would think that I wouldn't want to be deemed silly, but I actually like the mocking gaze, I feel like they're seeing the real me. I feel worthwhile because I'm creating laughter. R can't make fun of me though; it sends me into crisis and annoyance. I guess it's because I'm my most vulnerable with him.

I sometimes wear a black and white vertical striped jumpsuit I got from a brand that makes clothes that are like kids' clothes/children presenter clothes but for grown-ups. One time I wore the black and white jumpsuit on my birthday and R said: "You look like you escaped from Clown Prison." And I asked: "Why *Clown* Prison?!"

The author Rosanna McLaughlin, whose novel *Sinkhole* has a cover with a green, dripping *Goosebumps* font, writes in her micro-essay "You Are the Product" about feeling trolled by a pair of ridiculous clown shoes in targeted advertising on her phone *'Who do they think I am?'* she wonders of the algorithm, why does it think she wants 'white leather high-top trainers with red shoelaces [...] curled... like a jester's shoe, with a little golden bell attached to the tip'? The joke 'curdled' when the image of the clown shoes began 'to suggest that something sinister was lurking behind the veneer' much like 'a killer dressed in a childish costume.'

If language is a mass-produced balloon, and breath is the will to speak, writing, reframing through writing, is making balloon animals.

In this case: inflatable goblins.

(Did a foolish clown write this?)

GRIMACE

I'm back in Hastings at the foot
of both funiculars at once
good witch of the east hill
wicked witch of the west hill
duck into an empty carriage, the door slides shut
it gripes up the rails, the light sweeps and scans
my body. Then: the carriage rises, goes off-piste
fight or flight; like a fainting goat, I doze.

GRUNT

ON THE BODY, SEX AND PERVERTS

When someone touches me, they probably feel warm skin. But when I am touched by someone, I'm convinced their fingertips read me as clammy and slimy and scaly. I can't remember when I started feeling like this. Or maybe I do. Maybe it was during lockdown when I was suddenly on my phone all the time, it was like Gollum's ring, I would think I had put it down and then find it in my pocket, I would just stare down into it, like a well, like a mirror, and be shown svelte blonde woman after svelte blonde woman. Envy is the thief of joy, comparison is the goblin of contentedness. Daniel Ings, who plays Freddy, brother to Eddie played by Theo James (who voices Gelfling Rek'yr in *The Dark Crystal* prequel) in Guy Ritchie's *The Gentlemen* says in an interview that he's like a 'coke sniffing goblin' in the show, and when James queries why *goblin*, Ings replies that it's by dint of being paired in opposition with the immaculate James/Eddie.

I now get constant adverts for nose jobs. The Before photo always looks like my nose. It's like getting an emergency alert— *did you know that your nose and what it's attached to is wrong?* The Afghan-German author Moshtari Hilal writes in her book *Hässlichkeit*—out soon in an English translation as *Ugliness*—about the political nature of who is classed as beautiful, using her body as a site of exploration, her 'dense body hair, crooked teeth, and big nose.' (The German word *hässlich*, 'ugly', sounds like a hiss, *hisssss-lishhhh*.) In an interview with Edna Bonhomme on the Silver Press blog, Hilal sets out the framing of her book as making use of the notions and tropes of horror and specifically Frantz Fanon's concept of self-alienation in relation to the constant preoccupation as a teenager with being 'a person of colour who wanted to grow into a woman in a white society'—how ugliness is used to define those unlike us, those we reject:

I learned to observe and imitate what it meant to be expected, ideal and desirable in this culture [...] I learned to desire womanhood in contrast to the women that surrounded me, as in my aunts and my mother. In the logic of self-optimisation and assimilation, social advancement meant rejecting the women that I originated from, so it meant rejecting myself in many ways. Any good imitation starts with the looks.

I was an odd, unsocialised, lone little goblin as a child, apart from when I was with my younger brother. I sent my brother a meme the other day of Nicolas Cage and Pedro Pascal in a car together from the film *The Unbearable Weight of Massive Talent*, in which Cage plays a version of himself. The text over a disturbed-looking Cage reads something like *Older sibling figuring out they're autistic*, while the text over a laughing Pascal reads *Younger sibling with diagnosis who knew all along* and he sent back 'Hahaha!!!' in recognition: my brother was diagnosed at three; like many girls and women, I was never diagnosed, in spite of my hand flapping, twitching, issues with socialising, constantly feeling overwhelmed. Knowing that, of course, I'm on the autistic spectrum and have a form of ADHD (someone on the internet the other day said that 'ADHD time is goblin time') has eased my self-disgust and convinced me to mask less, masking is exhausting, this book is like taking off the mask, the fake nose and glasses, the clown make-up. As a child, I would shut myself away in my room when the sun went down with the lights off and the TV on, my nose inches from the screen, like a creature looking down a well or into a mirror. I was a sinful, roguish little goblin. My mum was mortified when I started humping a cushion in front of my great aunt when I was a toddler, and equally so when I snuck up behind her and pinched her bum in Woolworths, making her let out an involuntary shriek when I was about four. She used to take me swimming on Sundays when I was five or six and I once refused to leave the pool, pointing at her and shouting 'Stranger! Stranger!' to her cringing horror. I was a brown, dark-haired, dark-eyed, hairy little goblin. Children would point at the hair down my legs and my arms and on my face and call me monkey or, even worse, a boy. I wasn't like the well-groomed, mostly blonde and mousey children at school. I was feral-looking. And I was a girl, therefore a particularly furtive, gooey, twitchy, alarming little goblin. I often related much more with the beasts in *The Storyteller*—the Jim Henson-produced, Anthony Minghella-scribed children's series—than I did with the heroes and heroines. These fourteen adaptations of fables and fairy tales are filled with horrible things. There are fuming, goblinish devils and the dome-headed goblinesque Death in "The Soldier and Death"; the potbellied demon whose legs walk around torsoless in "Fearnot"; the awful trolls with rings through their noses who keep a young Jane Horrocks as a servant in "The True Bride"; and in the spin-off *The Storyteller: Greek Myths* with Michael Gambon on storytelling duties, Medusa in "Perseus and the Gorgon" has animatronic snakes for hair; the storyteller himself—played by John Hurt—is now rumoured to have been a goblin all along.

I felt more connected to the Straggletag than her beautiful alter ego, the title character in the episode "Sapsorrow"; a version of Cinderella with a young French and Saunders playing her morally ugly sisters. Sapsorrow is hidden under fur and feathers after running away from another kingdom because the law decrees she would have to marry the King, her own father (you can't get more patriarchal than that) because her dead mother's ring fits her wedding finger. She becomes the Straggletag, a servant in a prince's castle in a land far away, and everyone finds the Straggletag repulsive. The Prince must marry the Straggletag when the shoe Sapsorrow leaves behind at the third ball he throws in her honour fits 'her'. As the Straggletag she has a looser gait; a cool, lumbering, freeing genderless-ness in her dungarees. In Haunt Pitcher's thesis "Goblin: Microaffirmations, a Theory of Communication" they write about their brother adopting the name Gonzo (who they note is described as a 'whatever' in *The Muppet Show*) and then Goblin to refer to them as an acknowledgement of their non-binary identity:

> The term [goblin] was one I found validating due to my ability to use it to divorce myself from traditional notions of human gender. For me, it put the focus on my idiosyncratic and sometimes goofy nature, the strange faces I made and my periodic social gaffs. It reminded me that I didn't have to be broadly socially or sexually appealing—after all, goblins aren't terribly well-known for attractiveness or social graces.

Incidentally, you can tell *The Storyteller* had a music video maker as its cinematographer from its dramatic, dingy, woozy look—the various castle chambers, with light slanting through twilit windows and candlelit chandeliers, give you the impression that the androgynous musician Prince—who almost played The Goblin King in *Labyrinth*—might strut in at any minute. The Straggletag is often referred to as dirty, filthy, though there is only dirt under her nails from working. Her coat actually looks soft and carries mice in it! She has the same piercing eyes and throaty Irish accent as Sapsorrow. As Straggletag she teases the Prince, who longs for Sapsorrow. He seems at ease with Straggletag, even if her sarcasm and frankness go a little far sometimes for his liking, 'no one else in the whole palace, in the whole kingdom, talks to me like you do'. Sapsorrow is timid, frozen, perfection, flighty, delicate, silent. The Prince's reward for agreeing to marry Straggletag and breaking her cursed life is he gets beautiful, carefree, fair-skinned, hairless Sapsorrow (I just saw a young teenage girl proudly show her waxed arms to a boy at a bus stop), unsullied by past trauma and a sharp tongue. Straggletag/Sapsorrow's reward? Marrying a charmless prince who even pushes her over with the sole of his boot while she scrubs the floor for giving him lip. She escapes one befitting role for another.

The brother episode to "Sapsorrow" is "Hans My Hedgehog", about a hedgehog boy born 'ugly as sin, sprouting hair everywhere' to a couple who can't have children. The mother prays to have any kind of child, 'a thing made of marzipan or porridge', and has a hedgehog baby, who the villagers ridicule with the name Grovelhog and who the father finds beastly. Hans eventually leaves his family and the village, and his father only realises how soft his quills are when he hugs him goodbye. (This makes me cry every time.) When Hans is to marry a Princess, the Princess wants to break the curse of his hedgehogness. He tells her not to tell a soul that he takes off his quills when the sun goes down for three nights in order to break the spell. Her mother guesses that he's bewitched and tells her to throw his quills on the fire when he strips them off that night. She throws them on the fire and he runs off, only to be found years later by the Princess, who breaks the curse with true love, which... turns him into a boring, unbeastly, classically handsome man, like at the end of *Beauty and the Beast*.

(Such disappointment when the morose but charming Beast turns into a sprightly, uber-positive blonde.) How would I find love if I was always going to be a Grovelhog, the Straggletag? Would I, too, have to transform? I remember asking my Anglo-Irish mum (moon-skinned and black-haired like Snow White, green-eyed like the Evil Queen) how she knew my dad, a Maltese immigrant recently arrived from the Mediterranean at the time they met, was 'the one'. She told me that it was when they were in the back of a taxi and he ran his fingers over the hair on her top lip and then kissed her. The hair, after all, was soft. I'm basking like a toad on a rock right now in my back garden and the hair on my legs and under my armpits and on my lip is long and dark and shiny and silky. I like the way the hair on my arms and legs pokes through my tattoos, like weeds growing in the ruins of long-vacated castles. I have a new one of the Grovelhog on my forearm, softly spiky.

When I look in the mirror, I'm sometimes reminded of the meme where the image shows a woman's reflection in a mirror as a big non-plussed yellow-green scaly dinosaur-alien in a yellow 80s suit and gold necklace, where the text running beneath it says: *When you sit down in the salon chair in your plastic cape after a shampoo & wonder if you've always been this ugly.* This alien of self-alienation looks quite a lot like Greta, the 'female' Gremlin from the sequel to *Gremlins,* who has pouting, lipstick-ed lips, painted talons, long lashes and blue eyeshadow, a leopard print bra and mini skirt, an hourglass figure complete with pronounced breasts, and high heels. I found a Reddit thread where men wondered if Greta should be classed as being transgender or a mutation, because Gremlins seemingly don't have a gender, procreate through asexual means, and mutate from mammal Mogwai into reptile Gremlin. One reply, and then many replies onwards, are framed as saying that this is a conversation to be had with *buddies over some beers*, which I find really interesting because it's putting forward the drinking parlour chat, this gobliny realm, as a legitimate space where thought and meaningful exchange can happen, and then many concluded that the filmmakers would have considered the concept of Greta *very deeply*. I covet a model of Greta that can be bought from Forbidden Planet or the new style HMV (we have one in town) which is a mutant of HMV, Forbidden Plant, and FOPP, where she has green hair and comes with a beaker full of whatever it is that transforms her, along with a pink feather boa. It's currently on offer. I'm going to buy it any day now. (You can also get models of Slimer from *Ghostbusters* sitting down for a fancy meal with a bottle of champagne on ice; Alf with a cat sandwich and a Dictaphone; E.T. and a pot plant.) I can't answer the question of whether Greta is trans or the first manifestation of a sexed Gremlin. I think that primarily Greta exists in the film not for any kind of representation, but for laughs. *How funny that there's a Gremlin that's a girl—how silly and humiliating, what a novelty,* like when men at parties or in bands put on women's clothes in an attempt to be provocative (being a woman is provocative and very funny). She's also there as titillation. One of the guys in the Reddit thread/drinking table isn't interested in the argument, but instead declares that he wouldn't mind Greta 'all over' him. Monsterporn, if you don't already know, is a genre of pornography that includes fantastical creatures as sexual partners, including, *you betcha,* goblins, breaking through some form of the taboo of bestiality. There's a great Key & Peele sketch about the brainstorming meeting for *Gremlins 2* where any gremlin described is automatically in the new film, pouring water over the sequel because of how random it was, including its inclusion of throbbing goblin Hulk Hogan breaking the fourth wall. "Could there be a... female gremlin?" a writer asks Peele's sequel doctor. He responds frantic with excitement: "Just lipstick, boobies—bitch, you had me at little gremlin *va-jay-jay*... That's why we need a woman in the writers' room." (Keegan-Michael Key plays Skeksi SkekZok in *The Dark Crystal* prequel.) Rosa and Jake in *Brooklyn 99*—where 'goblin' is used multiple times as an insult—weigh up which Gremlin they would have sex with:

Rosa: When I was a kid, I had a major crush on the evil Gremlin.
Jake: Stripe? Are you crazy?
Rosa: Yeah, well I'm not gonna bone Gizmo.
Jake: I would.

(Andy Samberg, who plays Jake, also voices The Heretic, a Skeksi, in *The Dark Crystal* prequel.) Danielle Deadwyler, when asked what film she would take to a desert island and watch over and over again, says the first *Lord of the Rings* because she adores Gollum; "I won't do the voice," she says, then, five seconds later, *she does the voice!* Gwendoline Christie, who played Brienne of Tarth in *Game of Thrones*, reveals on *The Graham Norton Show* that her first crush was Basil Brush, and I know where she's coming from. A surprising amount of people on the internet say the cartoon fox in the Disney *Robin Hood* is their secret crush.

In the live action *Robin Hood: Prince of Thieves*, Alan Rickman plays a leather-clad (am I remembering that correctly? Who cares?) Sherriff of Nottingham, who near the end of the film tries to rape

Maid Marian. The film is officially rated as a 12 certificate according to the British Board of Film Classification. Under the heading 'Sexual violence and sexual threat' it says:

> A man pushes a woman against a table and holds her at sword point while referring to her breasts, and there is a sequence in which a man tries to hurry a marriage in order to rape his wife. He pins her to the floor and uses his legs to push open hers, but another man intervenes before the rape can take place. There are occasional mild sex references, brief buttock nudity, and scenes of threat [...]

The information provided here boggles (Boglins) my mind a bit, it's being naughty, full of mischief, *tee hee*. I feel like this description is a disguise, a smokescreen gaslighting me. Sentence A can be mutated into 'a man threatens a woman with sexual and physical violence'. Sentence B can be paraphrased as 'a man tries to rape a woman'. Sentence C could be 'the man is interrupted trying to rape the woman'. In order to keep the certificate low and therefore open to a wider audience, the depiction of the attempted rape would have actively been softened so as not to traumatise or disturb younger (and older) audiences, meaning that it's made into something farcical, humorous. We're supposed to laugh as the Sheriff hurries the Bishop through the wedding rites while undressing, we're supposed to guffaw when the Sheriff's mother gives him a pillow to put under Marian's head when he's pinned her to the floor (he gives a kind of eyeroll, and Marian gives a mildly irritated or bemused look, like he forgot to put milk in her tea), we're meant to chuckle when he camply shouts, "I can't do this with all that racket!" as Marian's rescuers try to break down the door. "You may take this body, but it will not be me, *it will not be me!*" Marian hisses up at the Sheriff but also us the audience, who hover over her in the position of the rapist(!). This statement feels more like a reassurance for us—*don't worry, it won't affect me*—rather than a defiance of him. And the finale: we see his hand fumbling below, and then he forces open Marian's legs in one swift movement, *hilarious!* I can be sure that as a girl I a) found Alan Rickman dashing and witty, and b) grasped this moment as unthreatening and exciting as playfighting because of how comically disarming and brutishly sexy Alan Rickman was.

In his essay "How Lustig Is It" Peter Kuras talks about Germany's answer to Robin Hood, the tricksy Eulenspiegel, as part of his succinct survey of the erotic aspect of German humour:

'funny' derives from the Middle English 'fon', meaning to make 'a fool' of or 'to be a fool'. When Anglo speakers say something is 'funny' it's often unclear whether they mean 'funny ha ha' or 'funny strange'. The German 'lustig', on the other hand, suggests neither madness nor idiocy, but pleasure and desire.

Kuras puts forward the performances of Klaus Kinski and Christoph Waltz as the embodiment of the duality of 'carnality and comedy' and how in their work 'the comic often serves as a kind of seduction'. Waltz makes us squirm with his charm as Hans Landa (to call a Nazi a goblin seems too straightforward somehow), as Kuras says 'you laugh at Waltz playing a Nazi and feel uncomfortable about the part of you that finds him compelling and attractive'. (There's little charming about Hedwig, wife of genocide mastermind Rudolf

Höss, in Jonathan Glazer's *The Zone of Interest*; she shrieks and broods in her little grottovilla on the side of Auschwitz, playing concentration camp cottagecore—the Taiwanese title of the film can be translated as 'Concentration Camp of Your Dreams' according to fellow translator Jeremy Tiang.) Klaus Kinski can play foolish and brooding, which enamours you to him, but for me he has always been frightening. Nothing could have prepared me for the Beast in Shelley Duvall's *Faerie Tale Theatre* series transforming into Klaus Kinski in front of a genuinely shocked-looking Susan Sarandon as Beauty; "It will take some getting used to," she says, when he asks if she's disappointed, he's no longer a beast—earlier she says the disturbing line: "I love to be afraid, with you." One of Kinski's daughters revealed twenty years after his death that he sexually abused her for the duration of her childhood and teenage years. Till Lindemann, the frontman for Rammstein, who has Kinski's corporality and has always played with humour and camp while booming operatic metal, has been accused of grooming fans for sex. There is a fairy tale quality to the downfall of these bad men. A documentary came out about the French actor Gérard Depardieu recently called *The Fall of the Ogre* about rape allegations against him, and French writer Michel Houellebecq was recently called a 'xenophobic libidinous creeper toad' in a tongue-in-cheek (try not to think about his tongue, cheek, any of him) article in Literary Hub about the 'defiantly unctuous French novelist-cum-provocateur' and his foray into porn on the advice of his wife to cure his depression. (I'm suddenly reminded of the frog prince Bart badly magicks in a Halloween episode of *The Simpsons*, with the enchanted frog vomiting and pleading 'Please kill me! Every moment I live is agony!') Fellow French writer Annie Ernaux fucks to get out of writers' block in her book *The Young Man*, her memoir about a passionate affair with a younger lover, chronicling a woman in her fifties with the fullest libido for both sex and writing. She writes about fucking *as if she would die from it*. Many people suggested Lars von Trier as a goblin to me due to his dubious filmography etc. (I'll never get over seeing Willem Dafoe, the Green Goblin in *Spiderman* and the cantankerous keeper in *The Lighthouse* wearing a prosthetic penis in von Trier's *Antichrist*.) His film *Nymphomaniac* where Charlotte Gainsbourg's Joe seeks out constant fucking often in dangerous situations and with life-destroying consequences is a metaphor for other kinds of addiction, but *also* for living to the extreme, *but also* for being a total artist—fully embracing one's life, one's desires; both put you on the edge of everything, make you an outcast.

There are three poems I know about our olfactory capacities being our lust for life. William Carlos Williams' "Smell!" (a title that both announces a theme and is a command, like *Nymphomaniac* in a way feels both a subject and an accusation) where he chastises his nose (*nudge nudge*) for wanting to smell everything because it might be off-putting to a girlfriend. Hugh Steinberg's "The Sense of Smell" is about smelling the roses and the cow shit as a call for vegetarianism and a warning not to underappreciate this sense as it tells us so much about the world, then there's Ian Crichton Smith's "The Nose (After Gogol)" where a nose runs away early one morning to sniff the world but is eventually gobbled up. In *Labyrinth* there is the Bog of Eternal Stench, and this, I don't know, could be a metaphor for shame, but I've never enjoyed poking the metaphors out of things I love, it could just be a smelly farting swamp. It was only when a fellow literary translator asked for synonyms for 'toilet' that I realised how evocative the phrase 'going to the bog' is. Incidentally, when Sophy Hollington did a series of mini-illustrations for the New York Times, the one vetoed drawing was a goblin farting through a rolled-up newspaper—a kind of stinky post horn. On an episode of *Chicken Shop Date*, SZA expressed her hope to 'swim in the swamp and collect methane gas with my man', a reference to *Shrek*.

What about the coercion in *Labyrinth*, a film often called romantic? What about David Bowie's legacy of seeking out young girls for sex? In an article supporting her book *Monsters: A Fan's Dilemma*, Claire Dederer queries 'Roman Polanski, Woody Allen, Michael Jackson... In the era of #MeToo what to do with the great art of scary monsters and super creeps?' making explicit that this isn't some kind of objective study:

> when I come to this question – the question of what to do with the art of monstrous men – I don't come as an impartial observer. I'm not someone who is absent a history. I have been a teenager predated by older men; I have been molested; I've been assaulted on the street; I've been grabbed and I've been coerced and I've escaped from attempted rape. I don't say this because it makes me special. I say it because it makes me non-special. And so, like many or most women, I have a dog in this particular race.

In the article she wonders, with genuine curiosity, what to do with all the men in the arts we know have committed, among other things, domestic and sexual abuse—Harvey Weinstein, Louis CK, John Lennon—when there is no magical calculator to judge whether someone should be cancelled and no stopping oneself being bewitched by the music of goblins. She homes in on David Bowie, who has somehow remained comparatively unscathed. After Bowie's death, an interview with groupie Lori Mattix rose back to the surface of the pond where she revealed her fond memory of losing her virginity to David Bowie when she was 15, and Dana Gillespie has claimed that Bowie had sex with her when she was 14. It made me remember being so disturbed by the way Bowie speaks about Jennifer Connelly in the making-of documentary for *Labyrinth*, which I found on the DVD I bought as an adult, because instead of his admiration for her fading into professional, paternal and/or peer-to-peer coolness, if anything his attraction to Connelly is suddenly flashed at us:

Apart from being *quite beautiful*, she's a really good actress and she's a pleasure to work with. One forgets that she's just 14 years old, I mean, she's really very mature.

Bowie saying the above converges with seeing a video of Gary "gross" Glitter quickly putting his finger to his lips to shush Roald Dahl's daughter on his edition of *This Is Your Life* for revealing that while he was living with her family during a stint of being unemployed, her sister used to bring schoolgirls home to come and visit him; and Robert "Goblet" Durst (*durst* is the German word for thirst) in the documentary *The Jinx* when he forgets he's mic'd up in the toilet and confesses murdering his wife and his friend: 'Killed them all, of course'. I get flashed on Instagram a lot. There are so many sexbots on Instagram. I often get an alert that someone has liked my story and up pops an arse, like the dick pic that pops up like a jack-in-a-box on Noa's phone in *Fresh*. A story I recently posted was of a photo of a maniacal ventriloquist dummy in a shop window and a random goblin man replied saying he found me beautiful in the picture and wanted to be my sugar daddy. He tells me at the end of his message, *No nudes!* You don't have to tell me twice, mate.

Goblin King, Goblin King, wherever you may be, take this child of mine far away from me. Toby is not just a baby brother in *Labyrinth*, but, you know, *duh*, Sarah's innocence. The infamous bulge in Jareth's pants, we learn from illustrator Brian Froud, was on purpose, it was, we read in a recent article in Shondaland, 'part of the Goblin King's devil-like allure', his look, 'screams 1980s bad boy'. David Bowie's Goblin King drugging Sarah in *Labyrinth*, which I once found so wonderful because she got to dream about dancing with and almost kissing the Goblin King at a ball, now repels me—and it should have always, seeing as Sarah literally smashes her way out of the ball by throwing a chair through the mirrored walls.

(I suddenly have a flashback of playing Blousey Brown in an amateur production of *Bugsy Malone* aged fourteen, where I had to kiss the actor playing Bugsy, who was at least twenty-five. There's probably a home video of us somewhere kissing, rewind, kissing, rewind.)

In *I May Destroy You*, Michaela Coel ends her tour-de-force about, among other things, the racist goblinification and date rape of her character Arabella by performing three alternative endings. In the trio of endings, Arabella stalks her rapist in the bar where he raped her then 1) she drugs him back, tries to look at his penis, and then beats him to death, hiding his body under the bed; 2) she considers him also a victim of some kind of past trauma and comforts him, stashing him under the bed; 3) she consensually sleeps with him to in some way cancel out or tape over what he did to her, and then tells him to leave, taking his doppelgängers under the bed with him.

I want to press pause on Sarah's drugging and real/ imaginary power dynamics, as Coel does. I'm going to programme a whole computer game just so I can pause it, bewitch you:

Instructions for reading:
Play the song "Art Decade" by David Bowie on repeat while reading this text. Read the text as many times as required.

<u>PLAY</u>   <u>EXIT</u>

You are still sitting on the floor with your back against the side of the bed, under which your Furby and Tamagotchi are gathering dust, the controller in the lap of your faux-denim sundress, cables cool against your bare legs. You are back at the game's menu, but too drained to press PLAY. A satsuma is just out of reach on your desk, where your phone lights up intermittently. After a minute or two, the menu's looped animation begins again, and you watch it through half-closed eyes.

[A thick black line borders a pink sky, dusky blue mountains, and a dark tree. The sun is permanently setting. The grass around the tree is sea blue, the marshland beyond is brown with glistening cream ripples.]

[Sitting at the base of the tree is Sarah, standing next to the tree is Jareth, the Goblin King. The title *LABYRINTH* and the options PLAY and EXIT float a little above the grass in front of Sarah and Jareth. The gilded bronze letters glint and sparkle.]

Sarah is sleeping propped up against the base of a tree, her arms and legs almost indistinguishable from the roots.

She opens her eyes, blinks, turns only her head. Jareth, the Goblin King, is standing near the tree.

He extends his arm, holding a peach. Sarah extends her arm towards him, reaching for the peach.

Jareth retracts his arm. She retracts her arm, turns her head away, closes her eyes.

[The leaves on the tree give a quick quiver; a shiver that runs over the tree's branches in a wave. Jareth's eyes are fixed on Sarah.]

Sarah is propped up against the base of the tree, her limbs stiff among the roots.

She opens her eyes, blinks, turns only her head, tilts it up a little. Jareth, the Goblin King, is standing over her.

He extends his arm, in his hand is a peach. Sarah reaches out to take the peach.

Jareth pulls back his hand. Sarah puts down her arm, turns her face away, closes her eyes.

[A trio of translucent clouds hurries across the sky as if on wheels.]

[Sarah and Jareth's clothes come into focus in front of the badly painted backdrop for a few seconds, they take on more detail, like stitching and rumples and sheens; a glitch, a previous iteration, trialled and ultimately rejected, but still embedded in the game's fabric. Sarah is wearing faded blue jeans and a pale blue denim jacket, Jareth is wearing black leather trousers and a black, flaky, almost scaly leather jacket. Their faces flicker too; the edits added to the faces of unknown models vanish for a microsecond.]

[Your eyes close fully for a second, but the lids come apart again, like magnets repelling one another.]

Sarah wakes up sitting against a tree. She shifts her legs among the roots. Jareth is holding out a small, round fruit: a peach.

Sarah's arm lifts up as if of its own volition, and she weakly waggles her fingers towards the peach. She almost touches it.

Jareth looks around; one look left, one look right, and hides the peach behind his back.

Sarah drops her arm. Her head tilts to the side. She's asleep.

[Five red butterflies move jerkily in a box formation across the marshland. Your eyes might be open; they might be closed. The screen and its scene are hazy and scorched. 'Sarah', or Jennifer Connelly, scratches her nose. 'Jareth', or David Bowie, sighs, turns to look out towards a marsh made of swathes of silk

being drawn back and forth by studio apprentices, drops his hip, gives
a sniff. They both blink, stretch. 'David', or Jareth, takes a sip from a
bottle of water hidden behind his boot, replaces it. 'Jennifer', or Sarah,
brings out a few rolled up pages of a script from behind the fibreglass
tree, scans a page, puts it back.]

Jennifer Connelly looks like she's just now flopped down against
a tree for a rest. Her eyes jump open and blink rigidly like a
ventriloquist's dummy.

She casually raises one knee, clasps her hands around her shin
and taps her foot.

David Bowie raises his right hand and right knee, then drops them.
Raises the left hand and left knee, then drops them, then repeats,
marching like a juddering puppet.

Their mouths flap open and closed in bursts. Jennifer Connelly
appears to be singing her #1 hit; the jingle she recorded for a Japanese
Panasonic advert released in 1986, the year *Labyrinth* came out.
David Bowie seems to be singing "Underground", the track that plays
over the opening sequence of *Labyrinth*, which peaked in the UK
charts at #21 the same year. They are singing soundlessly.

[The red sun turns yellow; the pink sky turns midnight blue.
A papery white owl arcs across the sun-moon before disappearing
into the blackness of the tree. Its yellow eyes flash once and then
vanish. It is once more twilight.]

[Jennifer is now 48 years old. She's wearing archival Louis Vuitton that could be a goblin queen outfit, an update of Sarah's white billowing shirt and white waistcoat with silver filigree embroidery. She waves to her parents, her husband Paul Bettany, and her three children out of shot. Then she's 14, Paul and the kids fade out of sight. They fade back in, she's 48. Then 14. David is suddenly 69. He is suddenly 38. 69. 38. 69. She is 48. He is 38. He is 69. She is 14. He is 38. She is 14. He is 38.]

Sarah/Jennifer can't lift her head. It rolls around her neck. She can't tell her limbs from the roots of the tree.

Jareth/David holds something out to her.

Sarah/Jennifer can't quite make out what it is. A blurry, furry peach? She licks her lips, and they are sweet and sticky.

She reaches for the peach with her eyes. She can see that a bite has been taken out of it. There are spots on her denim jacket.

Jareth/David kneels, holds the peach to her mouth.

Sarah/Jennifer takes a bite of empty space, chews peachy air. He smiles, leans in for a kiss. You cannot see if their lips meet from behind, only his backcombed bleached-blonde hair partially eclipsing her black hair.

He gets up. Her head rolls back to the side. Then it flops forward onto her chest.

He inspects the peach. There's a small beige worm wriggling in the bitemark. He puts the peach and its worm in his pocket.

[A lilac spew of lava erupts from one of the mountains in the distance. The lava trickles down like plant roots in time-lapse. You view the words on the screen from behind, in reverse, as Sarah/Jennifer does. One of her eyes, the only part of her that she can move, looks towards them. The fingers on one of her hands twitch, and then her whole arm jolts into the air towards the letters TIXE, lacking finesse and pixelated from behind, but they're out of reach.]

[The scene freezes. You come to as the colours drain to greyscale. For a single moment the menu options glow royal purple, like a goblin's tongue. The loop begins again.]

[You oscillate within a woozy waking dream.]

[A clock chimes thirteen.]

I see a lot of David Bowie/Jareth the Goblin King in Jamie Campbell Bower's Henry/One/Vecna in *Stranger Things*. Campbell Bower, who incidentally is a fan of Alistair Green, has a Bowiesque Thin White Duke about him, there is a tension between him and Eleven, or at least, young viewers can't help but find one as he towers over her, his face inches to hers, his voice booming to join him, that clock, surely sampled from *Labyrinth*, chiming urgently in the background, bringing out a Pavlovian response in me, I'm a dog salivating and gearing up to run. It feels like the same old propaganda for young girls lured by older men—the proffered eternity of power, the metaphor for worldliness. In a much derided personal essay "Age Gap Relationships: The Case for Marrying An Older Man" in which both the writer and the essay are goblinites/gobshites (she's just a wealthy socialite dabbling in writing, and the essay's about marrying rich and claiming feminism doesn't want you to live a life of rest and enjoyment), it's proposed that an older man will be your 'mentor' and that the perfect relationship is where a woman is always available: 'Ambitious, hungry, he needed someone smart enough to sustain his interest, but flexible enough in her habits to build them around his hours. I could. I do: read myself occupied, make myself free, materialize beside him when he calls for me', like Dobby.

Just as for a long time my writing was only a reflection and mimicry of masculine letters before I broke it off, I ruminate in the oubliette of my mind about the fact that my sexuality has calcified in the unequal and sinister dynamic of young girl and older man, and that this was specifically through 'family-friendly' fantasy films, which all include a coercive element between a man and young girl or woman, a wielding of power, a particular gaze I found myself reflected in, a regard of possession, submission, simplification. I've become uncurious and a little-or-*axolotl* afraid of my own capacity for eroticism, because of trying to evade the old ways and forms of expressing oneself. I'm talking about my body and my body of writing, both. And though I have been turned onto forms of writing that bring me energy and pleasure, I have not invested the same time or energy or risk in developing my body's knowledges. Did I expect Susan Sontag to have expressed the same feeling in *As Consciousness*

Is Harnessed to Flesh? I wish I could quote the whole passage, but this juddering moment will have to suffice:

> As a writer, I tolerate error, poor performance, failure. So what if I fail some of the time, if a story or an essay is no good? [...] It's just this attitude I don't have about sex. I don't tolerate error, failure – therefore I'm anxious from the start, and therefore more likely to fail [...] If only I could feel about sex as I do about writing! That I'm the vehicle, the medium, the instrument of some force beyond myself [...] An attitude of surrender to oneself, to life.

At 37, I don't know my role, I don't know my lines, I demand perfection from myself though I haven't honed my craft. Sex feels like a goblin, it feels separate from my body, and *lurking*. I feel hunched and creature-like. Sex Goblin watches me, judges me, waits for me to make a fool of myself: it writhes and dances around naked and pities my detachment from my, currently, *purely informative, purely functional* form. A meme showing a few geese proudly marching across green grass has a caption: 'Self-hate is over—we are all sexy now'. I feel like I need to take a leaf out of 'actor, comedian, singer and clown' Rosa "Green" Garland's playbook—her experimental performance *Trash Salad* about a leafy vegetable seeking out sex has her routinely joyfully naked and writhing in trash (one review recommended watching it with a Bloody Mary 'if only so that you can take out the celery stick and hold it erect against your crotch'). I feel like I probably need to spend the night at Frank-N-Furter's castle and loosen up a little, take some light-bodied lessons, some kind of workshop. Tim Curry's performance in *The Rocky Horror Picture Show* is mesmerising, terrifying, for its hypersexual nature. Who would play him in a remake? I can imagine Lil Nas X or Miley Cyrus taking up that mantle quite easily. (I now can't get the image of Lil Nas X giving Tim Curry's Devil from *Legend* a lap dance, just like he does for the similar-looking Satan in his video for "Call Me By Your Name".) I only watched the film *Legend* for the first time recently after seeing a film still of Tim Curry as the devilish Darkness in Charlie Fox's essay collection *This Young Monster* and felt totally overwhelmed by Curry's Devil (this makes me think of Devilled Eggs) and his attempted seduction of Lili. What would have happened if I had watched this as a young girl? David Bowie would have gone a whiter shade of pale and vanished, that's for sure. I mean, *my jaw dropped.* I was a teenager again. It's not a little bit on the edge, it's out and out erotic. This film went from dull afternoon snooze fest to dungeon porn with no transition, and not because anything sexual happens. The most basic but glaring reasons for this is Curry's technologically deepened voice and laugh, and the size of Darkness' muscular, naked and glistening torso. Nudity in itself is rascally, and nude photography has the rep of being a trapdoor to a dungeon. Sarah Piantadosi, in her photo book *Bone*, according to an interview, makes her subjects—not models, but writers, artists and musicians including the gruff-voiced Alli Logout of Special Interest—'sexy, devilish and subversive'. 'There's this cliché,' she goes on to say, 'of the male photographer and the young female model and the, "Oh, let's go over to my house and we'll take pictures" where all sorts of gross shit goes down' recalling the 'mountain' of 'disturbing' stories that came out about male photographers after #MeToo. (While in my first year at university, I volunteered to be photographed for a now defunct magazine for a fashion shoot, and, when me and the photographer, a friend of my then boyfriend, were alone in my tiny box room in halls, he repeatedly asked if I would go nude or go topless, getting more and more exasperated when I refused. Around the same time, a former male friend introduced me to Animal Collective through the song "Grass", which I think is genius, but which is now associated with being a tool for this 'friend', known for his tactility and camp humour, to groom and later assault me.) I once had a disagreement with a friend over the fact that I thought that women had every right to be topless in public as men do, but they argued that this couldn't be possible because women's bodies are sexualised by default. A woman's body is always sexual, whereas a man can be both neutral and sexual. I have never been topless in public; I would do it to be a goblin, but it would be misread. Being shirtless, especially as a sweaty man, is automatically goblin. Roasting, sweating Ray "Gal" Winstone in *Sexy Beast* is a sunbathing goblin, out-goblined by the small and wiry Ben Kingsley as Don "I'm sweating like a cunt" Logan, one of the most terrifying beasts of all time, who calls Gal 'a loveable lump, a loveable lummox, big oaf' and swears/sweats at himself in the mirror. Then there's musicians: someone online excitedly wrote: 'Bert from swede [sic]! So much energy! So much sweat! Kind of like a sexy gollum'. Iggy Pop must get a mention in this category. Margo Jefferson in her memoir *Constructing a Nervous System* tells us 'Black women of achievement with ambitions need to be wary of their public relationship to sweat', citing the remarkable sweating or more feminised 'perspiration' of Ella Fitzgerald in opposition to Louis Armstrong's profuse and performative sweating when they perform, and how transgressive and radical it was to see a genius Black woman sweating, something considered lowly. Jefferson's new definition of a minstrel speaks to facets on the gemstone of my redefinition of the goblin. She sets out in the section 'Rules for minstrels', using TV therapist Dr Phil, former President George Bush and the musician Bing Crosby as goblin case studies, that they can do things like not keep to social niceties, be grammatically incorrect, show that they're special, or simply act however they want to and be praised:

> Minstrels must have some performative essence (gestural, verbal, behavioral) that you (spectator, imitator and opposite) hold in contempt even as you crave its licence. The minstrel's behaviour attracts and repels you. Such wilfulness! Such shamelessness! Such presumption! You long for that performative license but you've been taught it's unworthy. Inappropriate. You have higher standards and better values. You're sure of that. But if, however briefly, you could act like that... get away with it... be rewarded for it...

Jefferson then magically transforms herself into Bing Crosby through her writing to see what it would be like, concluding with the declaration 'I'm Bing Crosby. I can get away with anything. I'm entitled to everything.' There are other obvious music goblins— I barely have to mention Lemmy, Ozzy, and Lars. Then there's the more nuanced and non-grim goblins. If you saw George Fisher, aka Corpsegrinder from Cannibal Corpse on stage, you would know immediately he's a kind of goblin, but in reality he's a kind goblin, a loving husband and father, close with his dad, and who spends his free time winning stuffed toys at amusement parks to give away. Keith Flint from The Prodigy—'by the accounts of those who met him, a genuinely lovely bloke'—known for his green hair and stare, had his goblinness charted in a chronological videography breakdown in Crack magazine after his death. In the 90s, Keith 'started looking less like Kurt Cobain and more like Alice Cooper', with 1992's "Out of Space" showing Keith transitioning from Disney Prince to 'gas-masked gremlin'. "Firestarter" caused a moral panic about rave on release in 1997, and the iconic video shows Keith with his hair spiked into horns and a 'demonic snarl'. There's Amy from Amyl and The Sniffers, wide-eyed, tongue wagging, jerky dancing, bikini, hotpants and muscles. Missy Elliott's Rumpelstiltskin riddling and magical transformations. Megan Thee Stallion and Cardi B driving everyone insane with their song about having wet cunts. A bonus: Patti Smith singing about pissing in a river. There's also Mega Bog, Mind Goblin (a mind goblin is defined as being a 'compulsive desire', that 'causes unreasonable distress to its victim'), Goblin Band, none of which are that gobliny, therefore they're very gobliny. The band Ravioli Me Away have a song called "Goblin Town" and the video charts three bizarre Brit caricatures brandishing Costa coffee takeaway cups, almond milk, empty beer cans and a mannequin baby going house hunting with a greasy letting agent from Gob Lets who's always on rollerblades. When one of them signs a house contract with a pen emblazoned with the Union Jack, she starts transforming into a goblin.

There were so many amazing musical guests on *The Muppet Show* who all got the chance to become David Bowie and reign among puppet subjects for a brief number. Ryan Gosling said in an interview that his cinematic crush was Raquel Welch on *The Muppets* dancing with a giant puppet spider. There's a perfect number with Debbie Harry singing a song with a gargoyle called "Me and my 'Goyle". She also sings "One Way or Another" and gives out punk merit badges for Robin and his Frog Scout group. I'll tell you who doesn't get any Brownie Points—the makers of *Poor Things*. I didn't buy any of that 'feminist' spiel, that Emperor's New Clothes stuff. I couldn't get past the idea of it being a bunch of old men willing to have sex with a vulnerable young woman who has the (literally transplanted) brain of a baby without repercussions or questions. The film suffers from the same problem as film adaptations of Vladimir Nabokov's novel *Lolita* (especially the later one with Jeremy Irons as Humbert Humbert) where it makes sexual abuse and sex as self-discovery for women fundamentally pornographic; the problem is the translation out of the interiority of literature, from the quantum possibilities and oscillations of the imagination when reading, into film. In *Poor Things*, reanimated mother-and-baby Bella Baxter revels in the abuse of power of these men and Emma Stone remains stonily alluring throughout her growing process from baby-brainhood to adulthood—we never read her as a child, she is always a woman. In the 1997 adaptation of *Lolita*, Lolita is neither described or portrayed as 12 as she is in the books but recalibrated to being 14 and played by a 15-year-old—but older-looking—Dominique Swain, presumably so no one would have their viewing pleasure disturbed. Even seeing Lolita feels wrong because she is a projection of Humbert's theorising, legitimising and fantasising. When Bella Baxter has endless sex with Mark Ruffalo (the worst English accent in film) and then becomes a sex worker, she gains a lot from it, but that we are watching what happens behind closed doors through the peephole of film makes her learning and her arc something else. In fact, when Bella reports of a sexual encounter to Ruffalo's scoundrel, we as viewer feel somehow cheated that we didn't get to see; it all gives us a taste for it, makes us greedy goblins.

Perhaps the best part of the film is where Bella Baxter learns to masturbate, does it at the breakfast table, spends the day in bed doing it. She learns how to pleasure herself, how to reach a satisfying climax, and, where I've previously said in an interview that narrative is like flirting, I'm going to go further and say that writing is of course like wanking, you're in control and building to something, writing is solo and non-performative and comforting, and speaking about writing feels like sitting in front of a room full of strangers and telling them about your kink and how you get off. I can't say what I need, what I like, what I don't. I'm afraid to be seen, to make contact. My self-esteem is at an all-time low, maybe I should take advice from Glamour, which put forward a new dating trend, 'Goblin-timacy', the concept of 'showing up as your flawed (but undeniably real) self.' According to this logic, we're all goblins but usually cover up this part of ourselves for fear of putting people off, in all kinds of relationships. What do I fear will happen if I showed everyone—both new and familiar—the goblin behind the mask? I never used to give a toss.

GATHER

The carriage catapults into the sea
a seal presses its dog face against the window
a jellyfish curls up and unfurls in my lap
trapdoors open beneath me, a rubber ring balloons
and the carriage bobs and rocks
I suddenly notice a glass box on the wall
break in an emergency
I give it some bearded mussel
inside: a joystick
do I head to dry land, or the wet way
where *cargo ships and cruise ships*
cabbages and kings
hover above the horizon?

GROTTO

ON HOME, DEPRESSION AND GRIEF

I've had a refrain the last few years since moving to Hastings.
'I need to get out the house more, haha! I need to get out more,
haha!' *Goblin Cribs* is a tiny, illustrated booklet by Anton Fröhling
described by the Glasgow bookshop Good Press as 'a home tour
of a goblin. Like a weird MTV cribs, in zine form!' The tour begins
with the goblin rolling back the stone to his cave, then drawing
back a curtain to show his dwelling, complete with bath ever-filling
with drips, a sink filled with washing up, and a hole in the rock
for his bed. If I gave you a tour around my house, I'd show you…

…my cat Ludo, who is currently trying to wrestle and bite
a green balloon…

…my cuddly religieuse au chocolat or "chocolate nun" (a small
profiterole stacked on top of a larger one) called Holy Moly and
my cuddly mussel in its shell called Moules Freak…

…my fake food collection—a wooden salami and chicken drumstick,
a miniature cheese and olive stand I bought in Naples, a salt dough
hamburger I made with a side of sliced pickles (the Belchers in *Bob's
Burgers* wear pickle costumes), soft felt fruit and vegetables…

…Grout, a cushion that looks like a grey torso with arms and hands
but no head…

…my plans to make a vampire marionette.

I want to make this marionette—more like Klaus Kinski's Nosferatu rather than Claes Bang's sleek Dracula, and nothing like puppet fanatic Jason Segel's Dracula puppet in the puppet musical Dracula's Lament in *Forgetting Sarah Marshall*—so I can make a short film where the vampire takes the funicular into Hastings Old Town.

OPENING

A CASTLE at sunset, possible location: BODIUM CASTLE, a half hour bus ride away. It will show him stationary in VARIOUS POSES in various rooms—sitting in a chair looking out the window, reading a book at a little desk, lying on the grass— and a CLOCK will be TICKING.

The journey on the FUNICULAR will actually be the journeys of both the funiculars in Hastings spliced together. First THE EAST HILL, which has a panoramic view of Hastings, and then it'll cut to THE WEST HILL, that goes through a tunnel down into HASTINGS OLD TOWN.

He'll aim to TALK TO PEOPLE, but he won't be able to get the COURAGE.

He'll eat an ICE CREAM instead. Maybe VANILLA with STRAWBERRY SAUCE.

He'll go and look at THE SEA.

He returns in reverse up the funiculars.

He ends up back at the CASTLE. He lies in his COFFIN staring up at the ceiling. The clock TICKS. The coffin lid SLAMS SHUT.

END.

I recently realised that it's basically the story of what I do every day, safely reenacted. For the last few years I've woken up early and gone for a walk into town. I used to love to lie in, I could stay in bed till 9 a.m. and it would be nothing, and as a teenage grotbag I would sleep the whole of Saturday and lie in late on Sunday, but now I'm irretrievably up at 6-7 a.m. and in town by 7-8 a.m. I know the few cafés that open early and sit and have a coffee and read or write. When I tell people that this is my routine or they bump into me picking up a coffee on their way to work they sometimes find it funny—*what are you doing in a Caffè Nero at 7 in the morning?*—or, to my confusion, admirable—*I mean, I go to the gym three times a week, but it takes real dedication to go and write every morning.* I can't describe it as dedication, it's more like an urgent compulsion to get out of the house. If I have an early morning online meeting and I won't have time to go, I get tetchy, panicky. The moment I wake up, the feeling is almost one of claustrophobia. *Let me out!* I interchangeably refer to it as my 'warm-up routine', 'procrastination' to hold off the day beginning, and 'entering the world'. I realise it's part of my struggle with not a goblin mode, but a goblin state I've always been in, one that is getting stickier by the day. Ralph Emerson, via

Naomi Klein, wrote '[a] foolish consistency is the hobgoblin of little minds.'

The start of this escape artist routine coincided with moving back to the coast during the tail end of the pandemic's peak, and my mum's physical and mental health rapidly deteriorating. The correlation to the former seems obvious; getting out every day and going to a café still feels forbidden and luxurious. The latter was one of the reasons we moved an hour along the coast from where I grew up and my parents still lived and needs a brief guided tour. When I think of my mum I think of her in her armchair. Always in her armchair, her illnesses eventually turned her to stone. Her armchair was her grotto, her entire world, with her things around her like satellites in her orbit— knitting, stacks of Stephen King novels, *Harry Potter* and *The Wild Thornberrys* on DVD (the dad, Nigel Thornberry was voiced by Tim Curry, the son, a feral Tarzan-like Donnie, by bass goblin Flea from the Red Hot Chili Peppers), extra wool, her copious medication. I think of her doing impressions of the *Clangers*—mouse-like moon-dwellers who live on green soup mined by the Soup Dragon and described by their maker as 'a family in space'—and the *Trumpton* Fire Brigade roll call—"Pugh, Pugh, Barney, McGrew, Cuthbert, Dibble and *GRUBB!*" with the Brigade often deploying the hose by mistake, and their Captain shouting, "No, no! Not the hose!" She loved all TV, especially horror films and kids TV. (The only shows I've ever seen make my dad laugh are *Only Fools and Horses*, with Del Boy the trickster imp straight out of a fairy tale, and *Gogs*, a claymation show about a family of disgusting cavemen—one episode is filled with mucus.) Mum spent long and short stints in psychiatric wards before and during my childhood

and teenage years due to schizophrenia and manic depression.
When she absconded from a hospital during my A-levels, I punched
a wall in the hallway of our house. When she tried to end her life
for the umpteenth time at a residential hospital during my A-level
exam week, I hit a wall and decided to move out of home and create
distance between myself and my parents as quickly as possible,
moving to Germany on my own two months later. Munich was a
kind of retreat, an uncontrolled and unsupervised rehab.

I'm on a John Mulaney binge at the moment; him on
Hot Ones talking about loving the fucked-up TV puppets at his
local museum as a kid; his fucked-up version of *Sesame Street* called
John Mulaney and the Sack Lunch Bunch where a mascot who lives with
schizophrenia is missing and David Byrne and Jake Gyllenhaal crave
attention during dazzling musical numbers, and the kids who make
up the kid chorus on the show reveal what they're afraid of, like
home invasion (one of my favourite bands, Murderer, have a music
video for their song "Piece of Candy" showing a goblin-like moon-
man marionette sneaking into someone's room at night through
the window, a running theme on their album *I Did It All For You*)
and being killed by their doppelgänger. I also enjoyed Mulaney's
other stand-up shows and his interview with big grump David
Letterman where he talks about how him and his brothers were
'little goblins' as kids and how his French bulldog Petunia is
a 'gargoyle' (I once saw a woman describe a giant green bust of
a pug in a shop window as 'absolutely lovely'); but perhaps most
of all his one-week-only live chat and sketch show *Everybody's in
L.A.*, described in reviews as a 'rickety curio' and often just as
being 'weird', because it made me cringe and squirm and laugh

uncomfortably and turn it off and turn it back on—it takes place
in an 80s-style (and therefore timeless—my dreams look like they're
from the 80s) living room, featuring the weirdest assortment of
celebrity and expert guests (with a Flea finale) and Saymo the food
delivery robot, Mulaney's well-behaved but sensitive Johnny 5/
Mr. Blobby.

John Mulaney, who has a Rumpelstiltskin voice and who
my friend Rita described recently as a 'vaudeville twink', speaks
candidly about his intervention and resulting stay in rehab to break
his spiralling drug addiction in his stand-up show *Baby J*, including
shouting and peeling off his shirt in front of the doctor who is the
exorcist to his possessed demon (I've never watched *The Exorcist*
as my mum would gasp every time it was mentioned, shaking her
head, my mum used to do a dramatic gasp whenever I would come
to visit, but the last time she gasped it was real because she couldn't
tell whether I was actually there or just a hallucination), mocking
the friends who intervene to try and save his life because some are
joining on Zoom or have issues with alcohol. At the end of *Baby J*,
he reads a crazy-funny GQ (Goblin Quarterly?) interview he did
three days before his intervention while high on cocaine where
he fixates on a local haunted house filled with 'ghouls'—he relishes
getting to use this word, recognises perhaps that he's the haunted
house. The Abu Dhabi-born, New York-based artist Farah Al
Qasimi's photography exhibition *Poltergeist*, which I haunted in
Berlin, is filled with ocular proof of a 'strange ghostly creature'
in everyday settings—a hand or bum dent on a sofa with a pattern
that could be floraline or coralline; a shadow behind obscured
glass in a bathroom door; a glitching collage of browser windows.

According to Al Qasimi, the exhibition is about the various invisible yet dangerous presences in our homes including targeted advertising and data mining. She was inspired by the 1985 horror film of the same name where a girl gets sucked into the TV, and her Instagram profile photo is Greta the *girlish* Gremlin.

But aside from a house of ghouls representing our inner demons, or the perpetual house invasion of technology, what if the house you grew up in felt possessed? In 80s-set limited series *Eric*, Benedict Cumberbatch plays 'grumpy' puppeteering icon and creator of *Sesame Street*-esque kids' show *Good Day Sunshine* Vincent Anderson (Jim Henson/Vin Anderson), whose young son Edgar goes missing. Vincent becomes convinced that the way to bring Edgar back is to make the puppet Edgar had designed and getting it on TV as a beacon—Eric; a giant puppet that's a cross between Sulley from *Monsters Inc.* (best friend to one-eyed goblin Mike) and Ludo from *Labyrinth* (vitally, Eric is a real puppet like Ludo and not CGI—though it's strange to think of who is inside the apparition Eric—is it also Vincent? We know that the artist Ron Mueck, Paula Rego's son-in-law, was inside Ludo, who he also fabricated).

Though everyone presumes Edgar must have been kidnapped, he actually runs away due to his parents' explosively brutal arguments caused by Vin's workaholism and alcoholism, and his mother's loss of interest (she is secretly having an affair and is pregnant from her lover). Edgar is not given a scrap of attention from his dad due to his toxic addictions, but he does get a scrap from the in-house puppet fabricator at his dad's work—a swatch of blue fur for Eric. (In traditional Turkish culture, blue and green were both called *gok* or '*sky*'.) After the particularly wild, screaming argument that triggers Edgar to go missing on his way to school the next day, Edgar's mother comes into his room to tuck him in (an E.T. figurine on his bedside table), and she cries while checking under the bed for monsters; it's actually a crying mother coming up from under a bed that is horrifying. (I never saw my mum cry when I was growing up.) One could draw a line between Edgar and Danny in *The Shining*, whose own parents unravel under the roof they're sharing and are the monsters under the bed (I think of Shelley Duvall as a version of my own mother, an ethereal presence whose mental health deteriorated over time). Eric the puppet appears to Vincent in real life, a sweary, belligerent apparition, a projection of his own self-critique, and he accompanies him on his epic quest to find Edgar. (In an interview, Jim Henson referred to Kermit the Frog as 'an alter ego of sorts', and moments before or after Kermit is made to say 'I do his outrageous things'.) Edgar would rather leave his home and live on the streets, among the 'hobos' his development tycoon grandfather—Vincent's father—wants to get rid of so he can build more apartments, the fire is better than the frying pan. Vincent draws fangs on a picture of his property tycoon dad in the newspaper that accompanies a report on him closing down homeless shelters, though not an ideal father, he did inspire *Good Day Sunshine* through this salutation to his son when he was a kid, before he became goblinified by capitalist greed. Eric can be read as a version of *Labyrinth*: 'Bring my baby [son] back, he must be so scared'. Edgar is going to be turned into a goblin if time runs out; he's going to be given to a paedophile ring to pay off a drug debt! Edgar went into the labyrinth of the sewer dwelling of the un-homed following after the goblin king, Yusuf, king of the 'hobos', whose graffitied tag of a crown has always fascinated Edgar. Edgar left behind a kind of map in the form of an idiosyncratic assemblage of city details that will eventually lead his dad to the centre of the labyrinth, these random scrawled icons are like the arrows Sarah draws on paving stones in lipstick in *Labyrinth* that keep shifting and pointing different directions because little goblins keep popping up and rotating them. Eric the puppet imaginary fiend is actually hardly in it, that storyline is (happily) usurped by detective Mikey's storyline. *Eric* is really about institutional racism and homophobia: Mikey is a gay, Black cop who must hide his queerness and the existence of his bedridden partner dying at home from AIDS; a Black caretaker and then Yusuf, a Black homeless man, are accused of kidnapping Edgar; the case of a missing Black boy forced into sex work is usurped by Edgar's case. The documentary *Jim Henson: Idea Man* came out practically simultaneously with *Eric*, and focuses on Henson's own workaholism, which is the reason for his marriage breaking down (he opted for living in a hotel and dating *no strings attached*) and which eventually contributed to his early death at 53; during the footage of his funeral, which was like an enormous puppet show, I bawled my eyes out: 'For millions of people it will seem like a death in the family.' His children (who as babies look like puppets in their parents' arms) all went into puppetry, TV production and the Henson company (the voice and animatronics for Hoggle in *Labyrinth*, for instance, was provided by his son Brian Henson; actress Shari Weiser embodied Hoggle), and I wondered if this was because the only way to relate and be close to their dad was through his work. My dad was always working, sometimes multiple jobs, and cared full-time for our mum. Though he's been retired for years, he must always be productive and doing things, he can only use workplace anecdotes to respond to life issues, he speaks in work metaphors, emotions are unprofessional and must be handled matter-of-factly.

After a year in Munich, I went straight to university in London, spending a reluctant six months back home after graduating, before moving back to London as quickly as I could. During those six months back at my parents, I lived in my room and wouldn't come out, recreating the kind of hovel I had lived in in Munich flat shares and student halls. Every inch of the floor was covered in clothes and magazines, I could barely open the door. You could imagine the Real Monsters under the bed reading the NME. I never washed the bedsheets, and I slept with books and laundry under and on top of the duvet. It was like Tracey Emin's artwork *My Bed*, the revealed grotto of many a woman in a hedonistic/nihilistic state. I needed somewhere to stay, but the whole house felt haunted, and I buried my face under the covers. My parents have become hoarders over the years, and my dad's garage has bled into the house; a stack of tyres in the upstairs bathroom with a car door in the bath became the norm. We all became Stig of the Dump (rag-and-bone father-son duo *Steptoe and Son* always fascinated me with their can't live with them/can't live without them relationship—when father Steptoe has a bath and drops pickled onions in the bathwater! *'You dirty old man!'*) and there were no Wombles on patrol, the whole place is now a cave of rubbish, like the scrapheap in *Labyrinth* where the bag lady shows Sarah a recreation of her bedroom filled with the toys and books and objects she covets. The bag lady stacks it all on Sarah's back. "It's all junk!" Sarah shouts, and the whole fabricated room collapses, allowing her to escape. I wish my parents' house was filled with junk from films and TV shows. (I saw that Falkor from *The Neverending Story* was found in a storage unit, and Hoggle from *Labyrinth* cropped up in the lost and found of a train station, the original Teenage Mutant Hero Turtles costumes have rotted so much their teeth are exposed.) My parents' house feels like baggage. Moving closer to the house I grew up in means that I feel its load on my back and my limbs and my neck again (today I'm wearing my green Toad Bakery T-shirt, which has an abstract toad/frog logo and the word TOAD on the front, and a large logo on the back that makes it look like I'm carrying a large toad around for a ride). In Luke Allan's gem of a memoir-essay "Death to Books", which is partly about how reading didn't help him through the grief of losing his mother, he imagines he was there with her when she took her own life: 'She's too heavy for me but she lets me pretend, sort of crab-walks over the floor with me.' The grief feels like constantly carrying his mum around with him, like a game they're playing:

> ...I spend every day giving her a piggyback from death to death. She kicks my behind like I'm a horse because she wants to go faster, but I can't. She finds it very funny and I find it very funny too but I never laugh.

My parents' house has bled into my own house, which I now, in spite of it being a good place of care and calm, long to escape. No home is safe from that home, it is a home from home, I half expect to peel back the wallpaper and find the orange floral pattern of my parents' house underneath. Just this week I watched the film *Hoard* about a girl growing up with her hoarder of a mother (who is eventually badly injured when the contents of the living room topples onto her) who ten years later starts bringing trash into her foster mother's house and reliving painful and confusing moments in her childhood—it was like looking into a slimy mirror.

Similarly, *The Bear* is about anxiety caused by one's upbringing and one's family and how, no matter your ambitions and how far you get away from them to become something, you will have to go home eventually—literally, mentally—and relive everything, watch those re-runs, ultimately pick up where you left off, and feel the flight reflex that got you out of there in the first place kick back in just when you have to go full throttle in the life you made. Carmen names items on his new restaurant The Bear's menu after traumatic family experiences—The Seven Fishes and a cannoli dish are both references to the horrific family Christmas we experience with them early in the season, with the cannoli being a twist in that it's savoury—Marcus the pastry chef gives it a bittersweet name 'the Michael', both a reminder of Carmen's brother who ended his own life after years of spiralling addiction, and that the restaurant came from the windfall Mikey hid in cans of tomatoes so his little brother could open his dream restaurant in the ashes of his diner The Beef.

In *Wanda Vision*, red hot couple Vision, played by Paul Bettany (riffing on, he has said, cheeky sprites Dick Van Dyke and Hugh Laurie) and Wanda Maximoff aka Scarlet Witch played by Elizabeth Olsen (younger sister of the Olsen twins) are seemingly living in hammy sitcoms from different eras, starting with a black-and-white *Bewitched*-inspired opener through to a *Hocus Pocus*-like

Halloween episode with an uncannily 90s feel. (*Too Many Cooks* by Adult Swim also mashes up genres of sitcoms—over a 12-minute long opening credit sequence endless cast members are added and it morphs from a family sitcom to a cop show [with a pie credited as being played by Lars von Trier], into a cartoon superhero show, all the while a killer lurks in the back of shot, eventually gruesomely murdering the cast as the credits continue to run, the glow of the clingy credits reveals the presence of someone hiding from the killer in a closet.) It transpires that Wanda has conjured this parallel, fictional space so that her husband Vision can live on after his death, and so that they could have rapidly-growing make-believe twins; it's a fictional, speculative zone to (re)animate her family. Why remake traumatic events every night in your dream restaurant? Why write about traumatic *durations*, over and over? Why bring back the dead, why fantasise about them?

The week my mum died last summer, I stayed at my parents' house so I could go with my dad and other family members to the hospital to visit her over the course of the week she was there. I spent the evenings back at my parents' house down the rabbit hole of a Facebook group dedicated to a *Labyrinth* convention happening that coming weekend. I had been following the lead up to it in the Facebook group for months, half considering going to it. People posted their costumes and shared their travel plans in anticipation. I noticed how messages in the group ramped up in the final weeks before the event. Some people hadn't received their passes, the car park had filled up, there was a rail strike and replacement bus service, information had been patchy and people were asking a lot of questions. The day before my mum died—which I didn't know was going to be the day before my mum died—was the day of the convention and, lying in a bed that night in my parents' old room, my eyes and nose itching (one half-arsed nosebleed) from the decades' worth of dust, my dad not sleeping in the room below me, I got massive gloopy blobs of schadenfreude from watching the disaster of the convention play out in the comments. The clues in the treasure hunt were wrong, it was a boiling hot day and there was no water, to get to the masked ball in the evening people had to traverse a wood and a grassy slope in the pitch black dark, the ball itself was just a bare wedding tent with no decorations, the bar was massively understaffed, then the convention organisers closed the Facebook group, causing the dissenters to climb over the barricades and open a new one in which to post complaints.

The week before my mum died—which I didn't know was going to be the week before my mum died—R and I and a couple of friends went to watch a screening of *Labyrinth* in the park by our house. While we were waiting for the sun to set so the film could begin, we talked about the booby-trapped maze of the art and publishing worlds. You feel like if you take a wrong turn right from the start you'll never get back on track, and that it's easy to forget that it's the friends you make along the way that keep you alive. Perseverance gets Sarah through the labyrinth, but far more it's friendship and others who want to challenge the Goblin King's rigged system. *Labyrinth* is partly about the power of imagination and finding a horde of friends, a gang. While living in London, R and I grew our found family, both out in the D.I.Y. punk scene, made mostly of misfits, and at home, in the warehouse we shared with a gaggle of others. There have been many depictions of flat shares, the quirky and the representative. *Rising Damp* (1974-78) must have been one of the first programmes about shared living. It started a year before my dad migrated to the UK. Landlord Rigsby (whose name I misremembered as 'Grimsby') forces the tenants in the bedsits under his roof to be his social circle. He's 'seedy and furtive', 'miserly' and 'ludicrously self-regarding', and spends his time perving over Miss Jones, being dismissive of Alan the left wing medical student, and baring his ignorance about planning student Philip, who is a second-generation Black British student. The Wikipedia page for *Rising Damp* has a section titled 'Emphasis on personal failure', where it describes how basically all of the characters are pathetic and cowardly, apart from Philip, who is charismatic, suave and sophisticated, and who time and time again makes a fool of Rigsby by easily convincing him for the duration of the show that he's an African prince. The writer of *Rising Damp* 'defended' the landlord character stating that 'Rigsby was not a racist or a bigot, but he was prejudiced and suspicious of strangers [...] he accepted Philip', and Don Warrington, who played Philip, said that the show 'held up a mirror to the way we were living.' *Spaced*, featuring best friends played by Jessica Hynes and Simon Pegg (who voices Skeksi The Chamberlain in *The Dark Crystal* prequel) has a couple of overlaps with *Rising Damp*; the live-in, boundaryless, seedy landlady, the pervasive sense of failure and Peter Pan syndrome. *Men Behaving Badly* gave insight into the juvenile life of man children (their girlfriends somehow enamoured with it), a kind of aspirational fantasy space where men could keep playing together in a flat-sized den/man cave, but where they're also old enough to smoke and drink. Clune's Gary is described on IMDB as 'relatively secure financially, but rather arrogant and emotionally immature'; he wants for nothing, and does nothing, lacking all motivation beyond his wants and needs. (Martin Clunes also starred as Fungus the Bogeyman in an adaptation of the Raymond Briggs book with the shonkiest CGI you'll ever see.) In *Broad City* we get two women being feckless, smoking loads of weed, causing mayhem to deflect from the struggles of trying to make it in New York. The description of Ilana Glazer's character Ilana Wexler—both women play versions of themselves—on the show's Wikipedia sums her up as an 'extroverted slacker', while Abbi Jacobson's doppelgänger/performative self Abbi Abrams is simply an 'aspiring artist'—both very gobliny identities. I can imagine them getting on with chronically unemployed stoner Nora in *Awkwafina is Nora From Queens* (Awkwafina—birth name Nora—voices The Collector, a Skeksi with snot constantly running out their beak in *The Dark Crystal* prequel) who, like Ilana and Abbi, depicts women (specifically from an Asian-American or Jewish-American background) wanting it all—'it' being the right to be irresponsible and ignore the future set out for them, something men have been able to be (seen doing) for years. *Peep Show* is a combination of these abovementioned goblin traits—a comfortable and arrogant hermit and his sly, extroverted slacker flatmate, who are not harmless and benign, but rather manipulate and creep the hell out of everyone. *Tiny Tots* is maybe the best show about a houseshare. There's an episode where Tiny stays up all night annoying everyone in the house by sweeping and doing the washing up. Tiny is an absolute green-haired gremlin, and he has the most rotten voice. The fact that Tilly speaks French the whole time reminds me of how xenophobic this country is. Can you see a children's programme, or any programme, on British TV having a character speaking a language other than English and all the characters understanding them? It seems almost utopian, whereas the majority of the world, the majority of families, the majority of homes, are multilingual, it's not that fairy-tale-like. I've changed my mind, *Don't Hug Me I'm Scared* is the best show about a houseshare. There's an episode all about what a family is, found family versus the biological, with the latter ultimately rejected (the Red One does a DNA test to find all the other Red Ones he's related to, but finds himself sticking out like a sore thumb, the Yellow One's dad prefers to gorge on fried chicken than engage with him). Shows that share mischievously difficult to remember titles—*Don't Hug Me I'm Scared, Our Flag Means Death, What We Do In The Shadows*—are all sitcoms about found family; be it puppets from seemingly disparate kids shows with different issues and crises; pirates with different pasts figuring out who they are; or vampires trying to fit in and their human servant Guillermo fighting his immigrant family's legacy of heroic vampire hunting to become a treacherous vampire. In *Third Rock from the Sun* the aliens find comfort in pretending they're a family, their home and the friends they make on Earth is what brings them together. Alf the Alien Life Form in *Alf* is a total menace who wants to eat the family's cat, but he also helps the parents lighten up. Robin Williams' alien explorer in *Mork and Mindy* creates frenetic chaos for his roomy Mindy before they become lovers. (I loved Robin Williams as Popeye, the green spinach-guzzling sailor with Shelley Duvall as his Olive Oyl, mother to their Swee'Pea—Williams went on to play the Frog Prince in Duvall's fairy tale series *Faerie Tale Theatre*.) Then of course there's E.T. who becomes a beloved part of the family, filling a gap they didn't know there was. (Have you seen the E.T. rip-off *Mac and Me*, a poorly disguised feature-length advert for McDonalds and Coca-Cola featuring an alien that is pure nightmare fuel?) Are these aliens preparing us for difficult housemates, difficult cohabiting partners, family members, children? Or do they just show all humans to be uptight creatures? I remember being off sick from school as a young child and watching *Alien* with my mum, who could never properly register my age ('did you know alien was GORGEOUS!' my friend Milo just posted online with images of Bolaji Badejo, a Nigerian visual artist chosen for his unusual proportions that were "creature-like", in partial costume; he was replaced by puppets in the sequels). As my mum lay on the sofa, I sat on a small, hard chair trying to zone out from the film, then realised a spider was crawling up my arm.

We make ourselves goblins by not poking the institution, the tidy home of power and knowledge, not challenging the status quo that is really taped together and deceitful. Joanna Scanlan played Terri in *The Thick of It*, an incompetent civil servant press officer who would clock off to the second, often not catch the obvious, and would openly lust over the Tory MP she reported to. (Scanlan also played Mildew the Bogeywoman to Timothy Spall's Fungus the Bogeyman—'a snot-ridden, farting monster'—in a more recent adaptation which likewise flopped.) In *The Chair*, the goblin is university administration and management, but also the institution as an unmoveable thing that causes trauma all over the place. Sandra Oh's literature professor Ji-Yoon Kim is finally made Chair of the department, the first woman and woman of colour to do so but finds herself corrupted by both the role and her goblin friend Bill. Senior lecturer Joan is plonked in a cupboard office in a sports hall because she's older and a woman, presumably because management want to force her out. When she goes to complain about ageism and sexism, she chastises the young woman put in charge of her case for seeming too young and for wearing too short shorts. Yaz McKay, the department's only Black faculty member who is wildly popular with students finds herself patronised and undermined by an older white academic, who is jealous, bitter, and who then doesn't recommend her for tenure. And where is Ji-Yoon when Joan and Yaz need her? Clearing up the mess made by fellow lecturer and crush Bill, once a cool slacker dude prof and now just a middle-aged slacker grieving the loss of his wife, who performs a Nazi salute in a lecture on fascism and literature and causes a furore Ji-Yoon has to clear up. Ji-Yoon ends up receiving a vote of no confidence and is removed from her position. She did it for Bill because she fancies him, but she is also enamoured with the system, she thought she could change both, but as systems thinking purports—the system isn't broken, it works exactly as it was designed to do. And following this, what could we say about Bill and his ilk?

[an interruption: I just had to run downstairs to the door to find the God Squad asking me if I've ever *thought about my future*, then the Green Party came knocking.]

There's a comforting Instagram account called @old.time.hawkey where a lovely man with a soft voice living in a tiny cabin-like mobile home in the Cedar Swamp creates a cosy atmosphere. It's a kind of roleplay where he welcomes you in with a "Hey buddy," everything in oranges and browns, old cartoons playing on his tiny TV set, he's our friend the retro hermit. He makes wonderful comfort food, Tater Tot pizza, pecan bread pudding in a Crock Pot, always with a side of pop. "There you go buddy," he whispers at the end of each video as he passes you/us the tray. The set up is the antithesis of Carmen and Sydney in *The Bear*; solitude, peace, making food just for yourself or your visiting 'buddy', not making what you love or what nourishes you into a job. The happiest Sydney is in the show is when she makes that omelette for Natalie.

I once wrote a short story about a woman who leaves her perfectly happy life behind to live like a hermit in the back office of a newsagent and who leaves her job at a swimming pool as a lifeguard to work part-time in a bakery so she can alleviate any and all expectations and responsibilities in her life. I half knew I was writing about myself when I wrote it, but at the same time I would have probably denied that I was. *Perfect Days* directed by Wim Wenders is about a man called Hirayama, played by Kōji Yakusho, who seems very content with his simple life living alone in a small studio and working as a cleaner of public toilets in Tokyo. He has an immaculate routine that is repeated over and over every weekday—wake up with the sound of his neighbour sweeping, pack away bedding, water plants, get an iced coffee from the vending machine behind the van, drive around the city carefully cleaning the bathrooms, eat lunch in a park and photograph the canopy of his favourite tree, visit a bathhouse, eat dinner at a train station noodle kiosk, read before bed—and weekend—wake late, drop off and pick up his photos, visit a bookshop, select the best photos to file away and tear up the rejects, visit the same small restaurant. The two weeks in which the film takes place show him having to disrupt his routine, having to connect and communicate with people, having to share his space, having to come to terms with the catch-22 of his life; that he has kept his life small and safe most likely due to family trauma, which, though it brings him a sense of daily satisfaction, ultimately means he takes no risks and connects with no one, remaining snuggled and swaddled in his grotto for the short-term returns of a perfect day that might ultimately lead to an imperfect life. Self-preservation means making yourself into a bobbly green pickle. The final shot is a close up of Hirayama driving while listening to "Perfect Day" by Lou Reed, his face oscillating between pure joy and pure sadness. 'How we spend our days is, of course, how we spend our lives', Annie Dillard says in *The Writing Life:*

> A schedule defends from chaos and whim. It is a net for catching days. […] A schedule is a mock-up of reason and order – willed, faked, and so brought into being; it is a peace and a haven set into the wreck of time; it is a lifeboat on which you find yourself, decades later, still living. Each day is the same, so you remember the series afterward as a blurred and powerful pattern.

Dillard wants us to find a balance between productivity or tireless action and being present, saying that a schedule and repetition is to fight against the void. I feel like I'm on a lifeboat having survived a shipwreck. Instead of sticking to a groundhog-day schedule in the hope it might save me, maybe I should throw myself out into the world. 'Our lives are often enriched by the bedlam that upends our

plans and shakes up the stultifying order we try and impose
on them' journalist Scott Tobias writes as the take-away about
Gremlins on its 40th anniversary, '[a]nd that can happen at the
movies.' Films, TV shows and stories are safe places to have
adventures in the safety of your own home, but they can trick you
into thinking that consuming them is living instead of applying
the messages you find in them in your real life. They are rehearsal
spaces, not just titillation to be consumed. The writer G. K.
Chesteron wrote of fairy tales:

Fairy tales do not give the child his first idea of bogey. What fairy tales give
the child is his first clear idea of the possible defeat of the bogey. The baby
has known the dragon intimately ever since he had an imagination. What
the fairy tale provides for him is a St. George to kill the dragon.

(A few lines earlier in this passage, he speaks of the fairy
tale's use for the 'the child or the savage'.) In an episode of *Bob's
Burgers*, Louise's favourite 'collectible', Kuchi Kopi, a green glowing
orb-like blob that is based on a fictional character in the Burgerverse,
accidently gets dented then melted by her family while she has the
flu. She becomes furious. She has a fever dream where she must go
on a quest to a fortress, representative of building walls up against
her family. In the dream a button appears that reads: *Destroy Fortress,
Forgive Family*. I felt like my mum was always cocooned in a fortress
of her own making. I was either the goblin trying to scale the
walls, falling over and over down into the moat, or I was fleeing the
kingdom. Margo Jefferson writes of Ella Fitzgerald's adaptation of
a musical standard into being about her own life, about her mother,

'the emblematic mother of those fairy tales she must have read in her Yonkers elementary school, the mother of Cinderella, and Snow White, who dies too young to shield her daughter from cruelty and neglect'. I had been listening to "Save Up All Your Tears" by leather-era-Cher—"Mom, I *am* a rich man"—for years on my MP3 player, but one night while walking home in the rain after my mum's death, the lyrics (Google them) took on a different meaning, suddenly they were about her, a silk scarf turning into a snake in my fingers, and I began to cry, and harder at the key change. When I first flew the nest, no one tried to stop me, and I travelled the land. Now it's my mum who's gone, will I get the key to the walled city? Jefferson writes about the pianist Bud Powell as both Theseus and the Minotaur, as hero and monster made through mental illness: 'Why couldn't Bud Powell find a way to be Theseus—slay the monster, defy the men who'd made him one, and outwit the monster inside himself?' Two things can be true: the Minotaur was a prisoner in the maze, and it did violence. We can mourn the minotaur, but we can also lick our wounds. *Labyrinth* is about the loss of innocence, about the importance of imagination, but integrally about grief. Sarah is trying to tape over her grief for the loss of her actress mother by rerunning her role in a play called *Labyrinth*, something I only realised a few years back. The last few years, I feel like I've been performing as my mum, winding up the same coping mechanisms. I've been doing a bad impression of her that's unfortunately improving every day. I've been in a grotto of my own making, one that surrounds me like slime even when I'm outside. I roll a stone in front of the cave whenever anyone asks how I am, just like my mum used to do. My nose grows as I keep lying to myself. I want to run away from home, and yet I want to feel settled. I want to slither off and disappear, and I want to burrow down in my bed.

There's a painting by Philip Guston where a man—Guston depicting himself?—is lying in bed eating chips and smoking while dreaming of a painting comprised of piles of boots, interpreted as referencing the Holocaust. 'I'm going to stay in this cave and see where I come out', Guston has said. He has a number of paintings that depict the Ku Klux Klan. They are both silly, ridiculous little figures, but also us: a Klansman artist paints a self-portrait; three Klansman figures, like ghosts, are on a school chalkboard. We're all complicit. The figure lying in bed is thinking about whether art can save the world, can help you save yourself.

Why am I writing this book? I need to break out of here. Writing is my pickaxe and shovel and excavation tool, it's my candle and torch. Writing is the double I built myself from scratch that can take me by the hand and guide me out from under the earth. When Weezer played "The Good Life" on *Everybody's in L.A.*, I really listened to the chorus for the first time (Google it, I'll wait). I want to feel human again. Alive again. I really do. I need to come out of my shell, or at least upgrade to a larger one. When do I feel warm and safe? I think I'm realising my grotto needs to be bigger than a bed, a room, a house. My grotto could be the world, humanity, people. Roger Robinson has a poem and collection called "A Portable Paradise"/*A Portable Paradise*, and I think of R and my friends as that grab 'n' go grotto; we can be anywhere and I can look at my hands and see *I'm a real [insert identity]*. I have to get the toad off my back, tour my hall of treasures collected during my self-inflicted exile.

Now I've said the words, to you, to myself, the mountain might start to shake. I've been keeping characters in books and films and songs trapped in a loop, an oubliette to entertain me, for far too long, maybe because this is what my mum always did. The same cassette in the car, the same VHS, the same stack of books, to simply start over, always with a new level unlocked, but with few surprises, or the possibility of becoming tainted and poisoned. (Ryan Reynolds, who plays Deadpool, calls old films his 'anti-anxiety medication'.)

The philosopher L. A. Paul illustrates the paradox of having a transformative experience through a thought experiment: 'If you were offered the chance to become a vampire... with all your friends having made the leap and loving it—would you do it?'

Paul explains that

> [t]he problem is pressing, because many of life's big personal decisions are like this: they involve the choice to undergo a dramatically new experience that will change your life in important ways [...] You know that undergoing the experience will change what it is like for you to live your life, and perhaps even change what it is like to be you, deeply and fundamentally.

I might always be in a goblin state, my mind might always glow green, but I can at least try shedding this skin for a fresh one. On a recent trip to Greece, I saw small ancient sculptures who were that perfect green I've always been seeking: bronze turned green through oxidation, their surfaces bubbly and Gremlin-esque like watered Mogwai; the green of a transformation, the green of a chemical reaction from exposure to air and water.

I've erased my years-old playlist. I've sent up a flare to get help to find my way out of these caves. I'm going to turn off the TV, get off my computer, put my books away, tidy the house, fill a sack for the charity shop, go outside, walk along the beach, once more make the whole world my kingdom. "It's so dark underground," Vincent says via Eric the puppet, "but I was scared to come up, and nobody told me that sunlight could be so pretty."

Destroy Grotto, Forgive Self

GIRD

I wake up in a ditch with a cat
sniffing me, a prickly lick to my cheek
I writhe up on my feet, mycelium has replaced
my veinage system
You there boy! What's today?!
I sprint—in spite of the long-term risks!
Notwithstanding my knees and hips!
In the face of looking absurd!—Home. I awake a second time
in my bed
a rough lick to my cheek, *sniff sniff*
my cat is snitching on me
to *me*, regarding
yet another daytime nap
she bites because she doesn't know how
to kiss. I start counting—one! *Ha-ha-ha!*
and by the time I reach eighty-six
I'm running out the door, chasing myself
undeterred by enduring harm!
Regardless...
*

GOODBYE

Like all mums, there was something magical about you
Your jade-green eyes
Your greenhouse filled with sweet peas
Your ability to pull cable-knits out of thin air
Your mysterious perfume in its purple bottle
Then there's the fairy tale about the kitten found
    curled up in your dark hair
The photo of you as a girl kissing a white rabbit on the nose.

You could conjure up
Birthday cakes filled with vanilla buttercream,
Profiteroles grown to the size of oranges.

Flying Saucers, those shells concealing sparkly sherbet,
    would transport you back to childhood.
A lifetime spent by the sea.
If we lift a shell to our ear, we might miraculously hear
A wooden spoon chiming against the bowl
    drawing a figure-of-eight ∞ in the cake mix.
Simply Red playing in the distance.
The clicking tinkle of knitting needles.
The echoing calls for you in a swimming pool on a Sunday
    morning.
Your laughter.

INDEX

QUOTED SOURCES IN ORDER OF APPEARANCE

INTRODUCTION

"Oxford word of the year 2022 revealed as 'goblin

mode'", *BBC News Online*, 5 December 2022

Goblins Wikipedia page

GREEN

*Cary Grant's Suit: Nine Movies That Made Me The Wreck

I Am Today*, Todd McEwan

(Notting Hill Editions, 2023)

"Return to Oz: I Killed the Nome King –

Doug Aberle", YouTube, 19 June 2020

"The weird movie only your family has seen",

Claire Manning @claireunteed, TikTok

"The Kidnap of the Green Man by the King",

Rebecca Tamás, *Caught by the River*, 13 April 2023

"Interview: Ian McShane", *The Guardian*, 9 May 2024

"Spooky story" and "Family isn't just the best

thing...", Alistair Green @mralistairgreen, Instagram

"Self Portrait in Green: a slippery snapshot

of a search for self", Jennifer Brough,

Lucy Writers Platform, 7 June 2021

Doppelganger: A Trip Into The Mirror World,

Naomi Klein (Penguin, 2024)

"Seeing Green with Megan Baker",

Hannah Hutchings-Georgiou, *The London Magazine*,

14 October 2022

"The Inauthentic Self", Lydia Bunt, *Review 31*,

20 March 2021

"Literal night and day...", Elise Bell @eliseybell, X

"As a Disabled Woman, Goblin Mode Doesn't

Sit Right With Me", Hannah Turner, *Refinery 29*,

21 March 2022

Slug: A Manifesto, Abi Palmer, (Makina Books, 2024)

"I'm calling it right now: sloth communism...",

Sloth Communism @DrRJChapman, X,

9 July 2024

Golem Girl: A Memoir, Riva Lehrer

(Oneworld Books, 2020)

"Shola von Reinhold: Ornamenting Biographies",

Fiona Alison Duncan, *Various Artists*, 21 March 2023

Disfigured: On Fairy Tales, Disability, and Making Space,

Amanda Leduc (Coach House Books, 2020)

"The Pearls of Pee-wee", Lloyd Grove,

The Washington Post, 2 August 1985

"The Undoing's Costume Designer Weighs

in on Those Infamous Coats, Once and for All",

Erica Gonzales, *Harper's Bizarre*, 10 December 2020

"Nicole Kidman's Green Cover-Up Is The Most

Divisive Coat on TV", *Vogue*, 14 November 2020

"How a coat from The Undoing divided the

internet', Morwenna Ferrier, *The Guardian*,

24 November 2020

GURN

"We're just normal men", @wejustnormalmen, X, 15 July 2024

"A Forensic Investigation into why the 'we're just normal men' meme fills us with such joy", Kyle MacNeill, *Planet Woo*, 23 June 2023

"Alice Munro: The Art of Fiction 137", Jeanne McCulloch & Mona Simpson, *The Paris Review*, Summer 1994

"My stepfather sexually abused me when I was a child. My mother, Alice Munro, chose to stay with him", Andrea Robin Skinner, *The Toronto Star*, 7 July 2024

Jim Henson: Idea Man, dir. Ron Howard (2024)

"Elmo is just checking in! How is everybody doing?", @elmo, X, 29 January 2024

"Young Palestinian girl talks to her puppet about the war in Gaza", @MiddleEastEye, YouTube, 29 February 2024

"Augsburger Puppenkaffee", Tom Böttcher @tomboettcher, Instagram, 29 July 2023

"Interview: Peter Friedman", *The Guardian*, 28 May 2023

"When is a nose just a nose? A brief history of non-Jews playing Jews onscreen", Marjorie Ingall, *Vox*, 21 December 2023

"Goblins, Jews, and Antisemitism", *Jewitches*

Women's Poetry and Religion in Victorian England: Jewish Identity and Christian Culture, Cynthia Scheinberg (Cambridge University Press, 2002)

"Leonard Bernstein's Children Defend Bradley Cooper's Prosthetic Nose in 'Maestro'", Marc Tracy, *The New York Times*, 16 August 2023

"Actually Lydia Tár did study under Leonard Bernstein, the late conductor's estate says", Gabrielle Sanchez, *AV Club*, 23 February 2023

"Maestro's biggest problem? Bradley Cooper's open hunger for an Oscar", Kyle Wilson, *Polygon*, 20 December 2023

"The Difficult Labour Relations Behind Commercial Animation", Jamie Sutcliffe, *Art Review*, 20 October 2023

"Internal Affairs", Andrea Brady, *Granta*, 8 January 2024

GOBBLE

"Fresh review – modern dating is hell in sly and gory thriller", Benjamin Lee, *The Guardian*, 21 January 2022

"One Of The Scariest Scenes In The Bear Is Half A Damn Episode", Matt Donato and Chris Evangelista, Slash Film, 20 January 2023

"I Made the Omelet From 'The Bear' and Yes, You Should Too', Nea Arentzen, *AllRecipes*, 13 July 2023

"The Bear's Omelette Has Chefs Divided",
Brit Dawson, *GQ*, 4 August 2023

"A woman, a couple of eggs and a bag of crisps:
how an omelette became The Bear's breakout
star", Stuart Heritage, *The Guardian*, 9 August 2023

Small Fires: An Epic in the Kitchen,
Rebecca May Johnson (Pushkin Press, 2022)

"Old Gregg", *The Mighty Boosh Wiki*

"An Autonomous Woman Is Inherently
Destructive", Nicky Beer, *Electric Lit*, 2 August 2023

Gāmboo!, Blue Shop Gallery, exhibition text (2024)

GAG

"Why are we so scared of clowns? Here's what we've
discovered", University of South Wales website,
7 March 2023

Animal Joy, Nuar Alsadir
(Fitzcarraldo Editions, 2022)

"Everyone needs to grow up", James Greig,
Dazed, 10 March 2023

"Various", Jeremy Noel-Tod @jntod
ideas for a new art world, The White Pube
(Rough Trade Books, 2021)

10 Years with Hayao Miyazaki,
dir. Kaku Arakawa (2019)

"Why I created the parody Twitter account Bougie
London Literary Woman", Imogen West-Knights,
The New Statesman, 31 January 2019

"Various", Bougie London Literary Woman
@BougieLitWoman

"Sugar and the Challenging Art of Genre Hybrids",
Tobias Carroll, *Reactor*, 21 May 2024

"Conan The Borebarian", Alex Chafey,
Screen Goblin, 15 April 2020

"i do not like mr. bean..." @serephfem

Black Meme, Legacy Russell (Verso, 2024)

Some Mothers Do 'Ave 'Em, Wikipedia

"You Are the Product", Rosanna McLaughlin,
Granta, 9 May 2024

GRUNT

Hässlichkeit, Moshtari Hilal, (Hanser Verlag, 2023)

"Interview: Moshtari Hilal", Edna Bonhomme,
Silver Press blog, 7 February 2024

"Goblin: Microaffirmations, a Theory of
Communication", Haunt Pitcher, Media and
Communication Studies Honors Papers,
Ursinius College (2019)

"Gremlins 2: Brainstorm, *Key & Peele*, YouTube

"When I was a kid, I had a major crush on the evil
Gremlin...", Season 3 Episode 17, *Brooklyn 99*

Robin Hood: Prince of Thieves, British Board of Film
Classification website

"How Lustig Is It", Peter Kuras, *Granta*,
23 November 2023

Kindermund, Pola Kinski (Suhrkamp Verlag, 2013)

"How did reactionary French novelist Michel

Houellebecq end up in a Dutch arthouse porn?”,

Jonny Diamond, *Literary Hub*, 29 March 2023

“Can I still listen to David Bowie?”, Claire Dederer,

The Guardian, 6 May 2023

Inside the Labyrinth, dir. Desmond Saunders (1986)

“10 Things You Didn’t Know About David Bowie’s

‘Labyrinth’”, Laura Studarus, *Shondaland*,

5 January 2024

“The Case For Marrying An Older Man”, Grazie

Sophia Christie, *The Cut*, 27 March 2024

*As Consciousness Is Harnessed to Flesh: Journals and

Notebooks*, 1964-1980, Susan Sontag (FSG, 2012)

“‘Sexy, devilish and subversive’: the photographer

detoxifying the nude”, Safi Bugel, *The Guardian*,

8 May 2023

“The Prodigy’s Keith Flint in 10 iconic videos”,

Sam Davies, *Crack*, 11 March 2019

Constructing a Nervous System, Margo Jefferson

(Granta, 2022)

“Goblin-timacy is the empowering new dating

trend you need to know”, Francesca Specter,

Glamour, 4 February 2023

GROTTO

“Everybody’s In L.A.: John Mulaney tries – and fails

– to revive the late-night talk show”, Ed Power,

The Telegraph, 4 May 2024

Poltergeist, Farah Al Qasimi, C/O Berlin,

exhibition text (2023)

“Various”, Kris Draper @old.time.hawkey

“Death to Books”, Luke Allan, *Granta*, 11 July 2024

The Writing Life, Annie Dillard (Harper, 1989)

“Gremlins at 40: Joe Dante’s untamed classic is a

love letter to chaos”, Scott Tobias, *The Guardian*,

8 June 2024

“I’m going to stay in this cave...”, Philip Guston,

Tate Modern, exhibition text (2024)

Transformative Experience, L. A. Paul (Oxford

University Press, 2016)

Tremendous Trifles, G. K. Chesterton (1909)

ACKNOWLEDGEMENTS

Goblinhood includes a couple of small sections from my pamphlet *Goblins* (Rough Trade Books) and a few lines from my essay "What if it's Shelley's world and we're just living in it?" from *The Shining: A Visual and Cultural Haunting*, ed. Craig Oldham (Rough Trade Books). The *Labyrinth* computer game hold screen passage was first published in Another Gaze magazine as "Oubliette".

Thank you to Abby, Barbie, Camilla, Chris, Dana, Elliot, Helen, James, Kat, Katie, Liv, Lizzie, Mike, Pia, Rebecca MJ, Rebecca T, Richard, Rita, Rob(l)in, Sophie, Tommy. Thank you to Hannah for letting me adapt your essay into a poem. Shout out to the Movie Watching FILM 2022 group—Alex, Flora, Fran, Jack, Lindsay, Lucy, Maria, Murphy, Oliver, Tamsin! And thank you so much to Nina and Will for editing and publishing both *Goblins* and *Goblinhood: Goblin as a Mode*.